Undeclared Work, Deterrence and Social Norms

Lars P. Feld · Claus Larsen

Undeclared Work, Deterrence and Social Norms

The Case of Germany

Springer

Prof. Dr. Lars P. Feld
Albert-Ludwigs-University Freiburg
Walter Eucken Institut
Freiburg
Germany
feld@eucken.de

M.Sc. Claus Larsen
The Rockwool Foundation Research Unit
København
Denmark
cll@rff.dk

Published with support from: The Rockwool Foundation

ISBN 978-3-540-87400-3 e-ISBN 978-3-540-87401-0
DOI 10.1007/978-3-540-87401-0
Springer Heidelberg Dordrecht London New York

Library of Congress Control Number: 2012938266

Printed on acid-free paper

Springer is part of Springer Science+Business Media (www.springer.com)

Preface

The Rockwool Foundation Research Unit has been carrying out questionnaire surveys of the extent of undeclared work in Denmark ever since the end of the 1980s, using a survey design which had previously been tested several times during that decade. The focus of these surveys has been on a part of the shadow economy which in Denmark is known as "sort arbejde" and in Germany as "Schwarzarbeit." A direct translation is "black work" or "black activities," but in this study we use the term "undeclared work." In the mid-1990s, the Research Unit also began to take an interest in the size of that particular part of the shadow economy in our neighboring countries. Was that kind of undeclared work more or less widespread in the Scandinavian countries than in Germany and the UK? And was it the same parts of the population that were especially active on the undeclared labor markets in these various countries?

The book entitled *The Shadow Economy in Germany, Great Britain and Scandinavia. A Measurement Based on Questionnaire Surveys* (Pedersen 2003) presented for the first time ever an overview of the structures of this sector of the undeclared economy in each of the countries concerned on the basis of surveys using identical questionnaires. *Black Activities in Germany in 2001 and in 2004. A Comparison Based on Survey Data* (Feld and Larsen 2005) was a follow-up to the description of the 2001 situation in Germany that was given in 2003; Søren Pedersen was again involved in the work in the early stages, contributing to the design of the questionnaire. A summary of Feld and Larsen (2005) was published as a chapter in *Jahrbuch Schattenwirtschaft 2006/2007* (Feld and Larsen 2006).

The present publication adds data from surveys carried out in Germany during 2005–2007. Main results up to and including 2006 were published in a newsletter from the Rockwool Foundation Research Unit in March 2008 (Feld and Larsen 2008), and a forthcoming study in German adds further data from 2008. These data from 2008 could not be analyzed in time to be fully integrated in the manuscript for the present publication, but we will refer to some main results from the 2008 survey as it brings additional insights of significance to the overall conclusions.

In addition to having a purely research interest in creating consistent time series of data for Germany over a period with changes in tax laws and when the government was making a special effort to restrict undeclared work and tax evasion in general, the Rockwool Foundation Research Unit has, through its cooperation with Professor Dr. Lars P. Feld, Director of the Walter Eucken Institute at the Albert-Ludwigs-University Freiburg and a member of the German Council of Economic Experts, taken a special interest in the relationship between deterrence and undeclared work and in the impact of tax policy and social norms on such activities. Professor Feld has been concerned with these topics for a number of years. In this project, he has helped to provide through new analyses a more detailed picture of the factors that are hypothesized to determine the incidence of undeclared work, including tax morale, tax policy and the risk of detection and subsequent punishment faced by offenders.

I wish to thank the German Ministry of Finance for funding the data collection in 2005, which extended the basis for comparison with 2001, and the Rockwool Foundation for providing the generous funding necessary for the project in its entirety. The project benefited also from the helpfulness of the Foundation and the interest they took in the work and I would like to express my warm thanks to the Foundation's staff, including its President Elin Schmidt and its former director Poul Erik Pedersen, and to the Board of the Foundation, headed by Tom Kähler, for the help and cooperation they have given to the Research Unit.

The interview surveys in Germany were conducted for the Rockwool Foundation Research Unit by TNS Infratest Sozialforschung, a private market research firm with considerable experience in collecting data for social science research. In this connection, Claus Larsen and Lars P. Feld were able to draw on the invaluable help of Gabriele Fischer, Arnold Riedmann and Harald Bielenski.

Special thanks are owed to Bent Jensen, Head of Communication at the Rockwool Foundation Research Unit, to the Research Unit's secretary, Mai-britt Sejberg, and to M.Sc. (econ.) Mark Gervasini Nielsen and M.Sc. (econ.), Ph.D. student Peer Skov, student research assistants at the Research Unit during parts of the period when the analyses for the book were made.

Some of the results from this study were presented by Lars P. Feld under the title *Semper aliquid haeret? Black Activities, Deterrence and Social Norms in Germany* at several conferences, in particular in his Presidential Address to the European Public Choice Society at its annual meeting from March 27–30, 2008 in Jena, at the Fourth Workshop on Behavioral Public Economics from October 11–12, 2008 at the University of Copenhagen and at the Sixth Christmas meeting of German economists abroad from December 21–22, 2009 at the University Heidelberg; under the title *Shadow Economy, Tax Compliance and the Democratic Setting* at a workshop by the DIW Berlin and the Hans-Böckler-Foundation from April 15–16, 2010 in Potsdam, under the title *How the Government Affects Tax Compliance: Survey Evidence from Germany* as a Keynote Lecture to the 66th Congress of the International Institute of Public Finance (IIPF) from August 23–26, 2010 at the University of Uppsala and at research seminars at Wuppertal and Nuremberg in 2005, Cologne and Freiburg in 2010 and at the Université

Libre de Bruxelles and the University of Frankfurt in 2011. Lars P. Feld wants to thank the participants of these conferences, workshops and seminars, in particular Naomi Feldman, Gebhard Kirchgässner, Wolfgang Leininger, Friedrich Schneider and Wolfram Richter for valuable comments and suggestions.

In addition, Lars P. Feld would like to thank his wife Susanne and his three boys, Immanuel, Leon and Bennet, for the time they had to give up in order to enable him to finish that project.

I would like to express great gratitude to the two principal researchers responsible for the project: Lars P. Feld and Claus Larsen of the Rockwool Foundation Research Unit, who has previously carried out research on tax evasion in various forms.

In carrying out this study, the Rockwool Foundation Research Unit has naturally maintained complete scientific independence in its relationships with the Ministry of Finance, TNS Infratest Sozialforschung and the Rockwool Foundation itself.

Copenhagen, April 2012

Torben Tranæs,
Research Director,
The Rockwool Foundation Research Unit

Contents

Chapter 1
Introduction

An old adage attributed to Benjamin Franklin and supposedly dating from 1789 says: *In this world nothing is certain, but death and taxes*. Likewise, it seems that nothing is certain in tax policy debates in Germany these times, but the claim to fight tax evasion and the shadow economy. During the last decade, not a single year went by without tax evasion capturing headlines in the news. The media appeared to be obsessed with the possibility that prominent people could be caught while cheating the tax code. One of the most heavily debated incidents was the Zumwinkel affair. In February 2008, an investigators' raid detected large scale tax evasion of German taxpayers at bank accounts in Liechtenstein. The investigations started with a publicity laden search of Klaus Zumwinkel's domicile, then the CEO of German Post. Supposedly, more than 200 people were involved granting the finance ministry the prospect of several hundred million Euros of additional revenue due to earlier illegal tax evasion or tax fraud. Delicately enough, the investigators obtained the information on Liechtenstein bank accounts by having the secret service buy stolen files for more than four million Euros. It has been debated since whether and to what extent the state is allowed for legal misconduct—if the action were unlawful at all—in order to detect or prevent illegal behavior by its citizens or on its territory. In subsequent years, this debate has been fuelled by further cases of stolen files containing information on Swiss bank accounts and bought by German tax authorities.

The new millennium indeed carried a change in German policies to enhance tax compliance by increasing deterrence. It has been the declared aim of that policy change to fight tax evasion in all its different manifestations—from undeclared work by cleaners and gardeners in private households, to more professional forms of undeclared activities, e.g., in restaurants or in the construction sector, to tax evasion in the international capital markets. Consequently, it entailed several different measures: one measure was the so-called "*Black Activities' Act*" or more exactly the "*Law to intensify the fight against 'black activities' and accompanying tax evasion*" (SchwarzArbG, Bundesrats-Drucksache 155/04a) in 2004 aiming at increasing both fines and the intensity of control. This measure has been supposed to decrease professional undeclared work but also small-scale

L.P. Feld and C. Larsen, *Undeclared Work, Deterrence and Social Norms*,
DOI 10.1007/978-3-540-87401-0_1,

undeclared work at the household level. Another measure was an intensified auditing by increasing the transparency of monetary transactions between individual bank accounts that in fact, though not formally, abolished the German bank secrecy laws; moreover the coordination of capital and corporate income taxation in the EU intensified, e.g., by the European Savings Directive in 2005 which implements a (partial) system of information exchange. Both measures have been targeted at income tax evasion in international capital markets. Deterrence was accompanied by additional policies like a tax amnesty in 2003, but also tax reforms entailing tax rate reductions in the case of personal and corporate income taxation in 2001, 2004, 2005 and 2008 and a new source tax on capital income and capital gains in 2009.

Like in the case of tax evasion, the fight against undeclared earnings and the shadow economy has been promoted by a broad-based publicity campaign. The financial control authority (*Finanzkontrolle Schwarzarbeit, FKS*) which was established as a federal tax investigation unit by the "*Black Activities' Act*" in 2004 has regularly published the results of its work. It has also advertised its activities with posters in dark threatening colors and carrying headlines like: We fight against the shadow economy to keep competition in your industry clean, or: Our job means for the shadow economy: You are not allowed to enter this construction site. Such campaigns are supposed to raise the awareness that activities in the shadow economy involve illegal tax evasion or social security fraud and that they are not a peccadillo—against a supposedly widely held perception.

Also, the fight against tax evasion is not a German particularity. Similar legal measures have been enacted by the Swiss federal government in connection with its "*Black Activities'* Act" of 2008 and most EU countries as well (Williams et al. 2008). The financial and economic crisis of 2007 and 2008 induced many different policy reactions—monetary and fiscal policy initiatives and new regulations for financial markets all of which had to be internationally discussed and coordinated. Interestingly and without a direct link to the actions of financial market participants which are responsible for the crisis, it entailed measures against tax evasion and bank secrecy laws—also internationally coordinated and mainly targeted against Switzerland, Luxembourg, Liechtenstein as well as small tax havens. The "fight" against tax evasion appears to be a ubiquitous phenomenon.

The most interesting question is whether these policies have been successful and whether their benefits exceed their costs. And costs do such policies have. The salaries paid to additional personnel to conduct audits and investigations may even be their smallest part. But also the benefits are uncertain.

In his *Economic Psychology of Tax Behaviour* Erich Kirchler (2007, p. 168 *et sequ.*) describes the pure deterrence strategy of tax authorities as a "cops and robbers" approach: if tax authorities treat taxpayers as rational agents only interested in maximizing income, they assume the role of "cops" aiming at catching the "robbers". Taxpayers anticipate their role in such a game and employ creative constructions of non-compliance using tax loopholes or accepting the risk of being caught and punished. They enter an "arms' race" with the tax authorities. As is well-known from game theory, such inspection games do not necessarily involve more compliance if the audit technology is enhanced, i.e., if deterrence increases (see, in general, Avenhaus et al. 1998, or, for tax compliance, Reinganum and Wilde 1986). They rather evolve into a hare and hedgehog like interaction (Schanze 1995). Slemrod et al. (2001) present interesting evidence in that respect. In a randomized controlled experiment, low- and middle-income taxpayers who received a letter promising an audit afterwards reported statistically significantly higher income, while high-income taxpayers reported significantly *lower* income. High-income earners may have better access to sophisticated evasion and avoidance technologies and thus interpret the audit as an invitation to play the inspection game. However, a similar experiment based on a large representative, stratified sample of over 40,000 individual income tax filers provided by the Danish tax administration led to the conclusion that "the effect of letters on *downward* adjustment is always close to zero and never statistically significant" (Kleven et al. 2011, p. 27).[1] They find "a positive effect of letters on the amounts and probabilities of self-reported adjustments to income and tax liability" which "reflect almost exclusively *upward* adjustments, and the effect on upward adjustments is always strongly significant" (ibid.).

Most importantly, deterrence policies may have unexpected costs because they could undermine tax morale. The tax morale prevalent in a society affects the individual willingness to comply with the tax laws. Frey (1997a, b) argues that the resulting intrinsic motivation to pay taxes is crowded out by deterrence if audits and sanctions are perceived as an unjustified intrusion into individuals' privacy. The justification of that intrusion depends on the relation between the state and its citizens/taxpayers. Taxpayers receive public goods in exchange for their tax payments with which they can be more or less satisfied. The satisfaction level affects their tax morale. Similarly, taxpayers accept policies of income redistribution the more strongly, the higher the perceived procedural fairness of the decisions underlying such policies is. Also, direct interactions between tax authorities and taxpayers affect the latters' tax morale. The way taxpayers are treated matters. Feld and Frey (2007) call this relation between taxpayers and the state a psychological tax contract. In the words of Kirchler (2007, p. 169), such a "customer-relations approach" aims at fair interaction between tax officials and taxpayers. Increasing tax compliance thus involves much more than pure deterrence policies, although sanctions and audits still play a role by supporting a social norm through its expressive function (Tyran and Feld 2006; Licht 2008).

In fact, the differences between the two approaches can easily be seen from the differences in the language that is used. Deterrence policies are usually accompanied by martial vocabulary: there is a "fight" or even a "war" against tax evasion. "Arms' races" occur. The media report about tax cheaters being captured at their homes and detained in handcuffs. This is indeed a "cops and robbers approach". In the psychological tax contract, intrinsic motivation and honesty are underlined. There

---

[1] The quote is taken from the latest version of the working paper available at the homepage of Claus Thustrup Kreiner available at http://www.econ.ku.dk/ctk/Papers/AuditExperiment_3rdDraft_v5.pdf (download on July 24, 2011).

is much talk about fairness and social norms and how they can be framed or upheld. Friendliness plays a role. In both cases, such words are used deliberately in order to most vividly explain the mechanisms by which tax compliance is affected. The connotations are obvious.

Given the two different theoretical approaches, it appears to be crucial to gather insights into the functioning of deterrence policies. Empirical evidence is, however, inconclusive. Experimental evidence speaks in favor of deterrence at first sight, at least when judged by Blackwell's (2010) meta-analysis. Higher sanctions or a higher probability of detection raise cooperation levels in public goods' experiments or tax compliance in tax evasion experiments. But there are plenty of experiments reporting evidence that other factors moderate deterrence. Scholz and Lubell (2001) demonstrate a crowding-out effect, i.e., the level of cooperation declines if penalties are introduced. Tyran and Feld (2006) underline the importance of referendums for the cooperation-enhancing effects of sanctions. Alm et al. (1993) emphasize the importance of fiscal exchange. Earlier, Fischer et al. (1992) even contended that findings from experimental studies are inconsistent. These studies hint at the importance of a more comprehensive approach including deterrence and social norms.

The situation is worse when considering field evidence. The problems start with measures of the size of tax evasion or any component of it, like, e.g., undeclared earnings. Measuring the unmeasurable is a difficult endeavor if those who evade taxes or participate in the shadow economy have incentives to conceal the true extent of their activities. Moreover, the main variables of interest—sanctions, audits, marginal tax rates, income—are often difficult to measure, too, or they are endogenous to each other and to the tax non-compliance measure. With full justification, Joel Slemrod (2007, p. 45) thus concludes his survey on the field with the statement that "the empirical knowledge ... is sparse". The very large Danish sample based on administrative data mentioned above (Kleven et al. 2011) offers new opportunities and important new insight, but "it is important to keep in mind that the probability of audit is not the same as the probability of detection, the parameter that ultimately determines tax compliance according to theory" (p. 26). Furthermore, it should be kept in mind, that social norms may differ strongly between countries and that taxpayers' behavior may differ as well.

In this study, we respond to the need of having further evidence on the impact of deterrence and social norms on tax non-compliance. The analysis is focused on undeclared work ("Schwarzarbeit") as a part of tax non-compliance. Undeclared work is also a part of the shadow economy. Chapter 2 is concerned with the definition and the measurement of undeclared work in order to demonstrate how undeclared activities fit into this broader picture. As Schneider and Enste (2000, 2002), Pedersen (2003) and Feld and Schneider (2010) have placed strong emphasis on definition and measurement, and have discussed the advantages and disadvantages of different measurement methods extensively, we provide only a short overview as to the definition and method used here. Chapter 3 provides a short review of the existing estimates of undeclared work, the shadow economy and tax evasion in Germany. This chapter serves as a reference point that first of all helps us to make a comparison of the extent of undeclared work according to our empirical results with those found in the literature. Second, the chapter enables us to put our results into perspective. Each method of measuring undeclared activities has its shortcomings, so that there are upper and lower limits to the levels of tax evasion or the shadow economy depending on the method used. This perspective helps us to underline the importance of the approach followed here.

This study is the most comprehensive analysis of tax non-compliance for Germany up to date for two reasons. First, individual data are used. Starting from an earlier analysis by Pedersen (2003) with data from 2001, the Rockwool Foundation Research Unit has conducted surveys for the years 2004, 2005, 2006 and 2007 with two waves of interviews in each year with the exception of 2007 where only one wave was carried out. This data set underlies our empirical analysis which follows an earlier preliminary study using 2004 data (Feld and Larsen 2005). The individual data enable us to look more closely into the characteristics of undeclared work and provide evidence on the phenomenon by industry, region, education and other socio-economic characteristics. Second, as emphasized above, Germany experienced a shift in the legal framework in 2004. The *Black Activities' Act* is a major turn in deterrence policy as it provides for a unified legal framework to cope with the shadow economy for the first time. Before, the legal issues involved were dispersed in several laws and were not fully comprehensible. Moreover, the reform increased deterrence considerably such that there is a chance to identify the effect of deterrence on undeclared work. It is a kind of evaluation study that we could perform although the high quality of our data does not suffice to conduct a matching estimation procedure. In particular, we do not have a true panel with particular individuals followed across time, but only four cross sections. Nevertheless, as the Federal Finance Ministry has not wanted to have a true evaluation study when the proposal by Boockmann and Rincke (2005) was not further pursued, our empirical analysis is the best that is currently available.

Theoretically, the analysis starts from the Allingham and Sandmo (1972) model of tax evasion as a portfolio choice and additionally considers labor market aspects and social norms following the theoretical analysis in Kanniainen et al. (2004). In these models, deterrence is crucial for tax compliance. In addition, marginal income tax rates, the level of true income and social norms affect tax compliance. In Chap. 4, we therefore discuss deterrence policies and the legal framework in Germany. Chapter 5 briefly describes the survey design. Chapters 6 and 7 are core chapters that enable the reader to understand the incidence and the extent of undeclared work in Germany in 2004–2007 as compared to 2001 in detail. Several descriptive statistics are provided to understand the nature of that part of the shadow economy as comprehensively as possible.

Chapters 8, 9 and 10 analyze the impact of deterrence, tax policy and social norms on undeclared work more deeply. In Chap. 8, we analyze the impact of perceived deterrence on undeclared work, while Chap. 9 studies the impact of the individually perceived tax burden, and Chap. 10 analyzes the impact of individual social norms on undeclared work. Given that the data base for this analysis is comprised of individual data, the subjectively perceived extent of deterrence, of the marginal tax burden and the individual social norms are considered. To identify the impact of deterrence on undeclared work, the time structure of the data set is used. We summarize the results and conclude in Chap. 11. In addition, a brief discussion is provided as to the validity of different policies for fighting the shadow economy in Germany. In particular, we point to the open questions in research that must be answered before any reliable policy proposal can be formulated.

Chapter 2
Defining and Measuring Undeclared Work

2.1 Definition

Undeclared work as to the definition used subsequently describes income from productive economic activities which are legal and taxable, but on which income tax, social security contributions, VAT, etc., are not paid, because they are not reported to the tax, social security or customs authorities (Feld and Larsen 2005). These activities are not only deliberately concealed from public authorities in order to save taxes, but also to avoid certain legal labor market standards, such as minimum wages, maximum working hours, safety standards, etc., and to avoid certain administrative obligations, such as completing statistical questionnaires or other administrative forms (Feld and Schneider 2010). The prices and wages paid are less than the full market price, and buyer and seller are both aware of this and obtain an extra economic advantage in this way. Only activities which violate the German law against "Schwarzarbeit" are included in the definition. A direct translation of "Schwarzarbeit" is "black work" or "black activities", but in this report we use the term "undeclared work" for "Schwarzarbeit".

Trade in goods and services, payments in cash and in kind, and exchanges of goods or services between friends and neighbors are included. Evasion which benefits only one side (capital income tax evasion, sales at full market price that are not entered into the cash register, etc.) is not included. Undeclared work thus is one part of the domestic product which is not regularly or explicitly accounted for in the national accounts statistics, but has to be estimated. However, it does not include any illegal activities such as drug dealing, prostitution, gambling and so on. While we may seem to have used the terms "undeclared work", "the shadow economy" and "undeclared earnings" interchangeably in the introductory chapter and also embedded the discussion into the broader tax evasion context, we are well aware of the fact that they may mean different things, although the boundaries between these different underground economic activities cannot be sharply defined. What is important for our purposes is the fact that the basic theoretical

L.P. Feld and C. Larsen, *Undeclared Work, Deterrence and Social Norms*,
DOI 10.1007/978-3-540-87401-0_2,

underpinnings of these different activities remain the same and are obtained from the economic theory of crime (Becker 1968).

Undeclared work can be distinguished from other parts of the shadow economy by the fact that activities that are in themselves illegal are not included. For example, drug dealing is part of the shadow economy but not part of undeclared work. Undeclared work involves tax evasion and evasion of social security contributions, but it does not make up the whole amount of tax evasion in a country because evasion in connection with sales and services at full market price and the non-declaration of any form of capital or transfer income are not counted. Thus, undeclared work mainly involves labor as a production factor, only considering basically respectable activities that could just as well take place in the official economy. For example, work in the construction sector that is not declared to the tax administration, or childcare the income from which is undeclared, or work as a waiter/waitress in the tourist industry which is not officially notified to the tax authorities, all belong to undeclared work. Table 2.1 summarizes such informal or non-declared activities.

Obviously, not all informal economic activities are taxable according to German law. Do-it-yourself work is not, but, for example, (work paid with) reciprocal favors may be if there is a binding agreement between the parties or if the value is substantial and would normally involve a binding agreement (Pedersen 2003). The definition of undeclared work used in this report is not a canonical one because there is no canonical definition. However, it appears to be a useful definition.

2.2 Methods of "Measuring the Unmeasurable"

In particular, this definition is useful for the way we measure undeclared work. There is a broad discussion in the literature as to the most acceptable way of "measuring the unmeasurable". Because the discussions by Thomas (1999),

Table 2.1 A taxonomy of informal (non-declared) economic activities

Type of activity	Monetary transactions		Non-monetary transactions	
Illegal activities	Trade in stolen goods; drug dealing and manufacturing; prostitution; gambling; smuggling; fraud; etc.		Barter of drugs, stolen goods, smuggling, etc; produce or growing drugs for own use; theft for own use	
	Tax evasion	Tax avoidance	Tax evasion	Tax avoidance
Legal activities	Unreported income from self-employment; wages, salaries and assets from unreported work related to legal services and goods	Employee discounts, fringe benefits	Barter of legal services and goods	All do-it-yourself work and neighbor help

Source: The table is from Feld and Schneider (2010, p. 112) but with a slightly changed heading

Schneider and Enste (2000, 2002), Pedersen (2003), Lyssiotou et al. (2004) and Feld and Schneider (2010) are already very extensive, it is not necessary to provide a comprehensive overview in this report. Still, a few remarks are warranted.

2.2.1 Indirect Methods of Measurement

There are indirect and direct methods of measurement. The indirect methods use macroeconomic data to assess the extent of tax evasion, the shadow economy or undeclared work. The first method starts from the observation that there must be something like tax evasion going on if people in an economy buy more products and services than they officially have money for, given their earned income according to income tax declarations. In the circular flow model of national accounting, the income measure should be the same as the expenditure measure of the domestic product. Of course, statistical discrepancies might occur just because the quality of the data is insufficient. This may obtain particularly in international transactions. Still, it is highly implausible that these statistical discrepancies should increase substantially over time. If both measures of the domestic product are independently accounted for in such a way that no adjustments are made inside the statistical office, the gap between income measures can be used as an indirect measure of tax evasion, the shadow economy or undeclared work. This method is called the income gap method and has been applied in particular in the studies on Swiss tax evasion by Weck-Hannemann and Pommerehne (1989), Pommerehne and Weck-Hannemann (1996), Pommerehne and Frey (1992), Frey (1997b), Feld and Frey (2002a, 2005) and Frey and Feld (2002). Other examples of estimates based on various discrepancies and residuals are Larsen (2002) and Viby Mogensen (2003), who estimate unreported personal income by examining discrepancies between Danish national accounts, including the undeclared work, and the primary tax statistics, which solely reflect the formal economy. The method was adopted by the Danish Tax and Customs Administration which continued the time series. In a similar fashion, the official participation rate in the labor market can be contrasted with the actual employment rate according to independent sources (Pedersen 2003).

The second indirect measurement method is based on monetary approaches. The first of these approaches is called the transactions approach and was developed by Feige (1989). This method starts from the famous Fisher equation of the quantity theory of money. Relating total nominal GNP to total transactions, the GNP of the shadow economy can be obtained by subtracting official GNP from total nominal GNP, assuming a base year in which the ratio of total transactions to total nominal GNP was normal, i.e. no shadow economy existed. The second monetary method, often used by Schneider (2004a, b) and also by Kirchgässner (1983), is the currency demand approach. This method starts from the premise that transactions in the shadow economy as well as undeclared work involve cash payments to a larger extent than transactions in the official economy, in order to leave no accounting traces. The size of the shadow economy is then simply inferred by simulating currency demand with and without tax variables.

The third indirect method is the electricity consumption method (Schneider and Enste 2000, 2002). Assuming that electricity serves as a good physical indicator of overall economic activity and that the estimate of electricity to GDP elasticity is close to one, a calculation can be made of how large the actual total GDP of a country is. The difference from official GDP provides an estimate of the shadow economy. Schneider and Enste (2000, 2002) also describe the more sophisticated econometric method developed by Lackó (1998), which also uses household consumption of electricity.

The fourth indirect method is the hidden variable approach as introduced by Frey and Weck-Hannemann (1984) and Weck-Hannemann et al. (1984). Three or four macroeconomic indicators, usually the participation rate, the growth of real GDP, currency demand and working hours, are used as indicator variables for the shadow economy and linked to explanatory variables such as different tax rates or the regulatory burden using LISREL techniques (structural causal modeling techniques or the MIMIC approach). In fact, this approach is a synthesis of different elements of other approaches, because it combines the currency demand approach, the income discrepancy method, and the employment approach. In the collaboration with Körner and Strotmann (2004) and in Feld and Schneider (2010), one of the present writers has also worked with the hidden variable approach in studying the shadow economy.

2.2.2 Direct Methods of Measurement

There are three main direct methods. In the first, undeclared work is measured by using surveys in which individuals are directly asked whether they carry out any undeclared work, either for cash payments or payments in kind. This is the method applied by Pedersen (2003) and Feld and Larsen (2005) for Germany (and other countries). According to Schneider and Enste (2000), this method is most popular in the Scandinavian countries.

The second direct method is based on actual tax auditing and other compliance methods (Engel and Hines 1999). It is the method of choice applied by the U.S. Internal Revenue Service (IRS). From 1963 to 1988, the IRS has conducted a periodic tax audit called the Taxpayer Compliance Measurement Program (TCMP). It was cancelled in 1995 because of complaints in Congress, but followed by the National Research Program (NRP) in 2001. Using a random sample of individual income taxpayers, the IRS has measured their net understatement of income, overstatement of deductions and exemptions, etc., and used the outcome to calculate tax evasion for the whole population. Less frequently, a similar procedure has been used for non-filers, whereby the IRS applies a tax gap method to micro-data on actual tax cheaters by calculating the discrepancy between the declared income and actual income of randomly audited individuals. These data have been extensively analyzed by U.S. research teams (see the survey by Andreoni et al. 1998; Slemrod and Yitzhaki 2002; Slemrod 2007). For a comprehensive Danish taxpayer compliance study, see the above-mentioned study by Kleven et al. (2011).

The third direct method aims at measuring tax morale instead of tax evasion. It could either be summarized under the direct methods to measure tax morale or under the indirect methods to assess tax evasion. In applying this method, the World Values Survey asks a representative sample of individuals to evaluate the evasion of taxes on an ordinal scale from 1 to 10, the higher value on the scale representing the greater acceptance of that action. Five series of this worldwide survey have already been conducted for Germany, i.e. for the years 1981, 1990, 1997, 1999 and 2006. Torgler (2003) has explored these data extensively in his Ph.D. thesis and has published analyses for almost every country for which these data have been collected. Feld et al. (2009) analyze the WVS tax morale data for (West and East) Germany until 1999. Körner and Strotmann (2004) have studied the same data. Similar data have been collected by the Rockwool Foundation Research Unit (Feld and Larsen 2005, 2008 and for the present study) and in a special Eurobarometer survey (2007).

In addition to direct and indirect methods, experimental methods could be considered as another possible approach to analyzing tax compliance. Laboratory experiments provide for the cleanest environment to analyze the theoretical predictions of the economic analysis of tax compliance. However, as is often the case in laboratory experiments in the social sciences, the high internal validity of the experiment is obtained in exchange for the price of a low external validity. The artificial conditions created in the lab do not allow for a full transfer of the results to the real world. With respect to the measurement of the extent of undeclared work or of tax evasion, this becomes clear immediately: experimental methods enable the analysis of the impact of deterrence on tax compliance, but do not allow for a measurement of the size of tax evasion. James Alm in particular has advocated the experimental analysis of tax compliance (see Alm et al. 1992a, b, 1992c, 1993, 1999, see also Torgler 2002, 2007 and Blackwell 2010 for surveys). There are also analyses by researchers from German-speaking countries who emphasize the experimental approach to tax compliance (Güth and Mackscheidt 1985; Feld and Tyran 2002; Güth et al. 2005).

2.3 A Comparison of Methods of Measurement

It is common knowledge in the scientific community that none of these measurement methods is without disadvantages. Any method has its flaws. The survey approach (the first direct measurement method described above) is sensitive to the formulation of the questions, and may not capture the total amount of undeclared work because the participants in the survey simply do not tell the truth. Even in face-to-face interviews, which promote the greatest degree of participation in the survey, a participant may lie. The incentives to reply truthfully to the questionnaire are increased if the interviewer can credibly promise to handle the information confidentially. The advantage of the survey method lies in the additional details that can be obtained from the respondents, so that a very well differentiated analysis of undeclared work is possible. The survey method thus measures a lower limit of undeclared work in the economy.

The tax auditing method, as the second direct method mentioned above, also has its drawbacks. Tax compliance data are obtained from a restricted sample of the population, because the selection for audit is based on the properties of the tax returns submitted to the tax office. In addition, those taxpayers identified as tax cheaters could well reflect only the tip of the iceberg, because it is highly improbable that tax authorities would detect all tax cheaters even if they wanted to. Those taxpayers audited by the IRS certainly have an incentive to conceal any tax cheating, because they must believe that they face the threat of punishment if they are detected.

Indirect methods also all have their flaws. To name but a few: the survey of individual tax morale only measures hypothetical tax morale and not real tax compliance; the income gap method may only capture statistical errors; the monetary methods may over-estimate the rationality of the money market, and in addition, many transactions in the shadow economy take place without cash payments; the electricity approach is too dependent on the assumption that the shadow economy involves the use of electricity; and so on. The advantage of indirect methods is that they may circumvent all the strategic problems that emerge if individuals are directly approached with questions about or even audits of their tax honesty. It could thus perhaps be argued that the macroeconomic indirect methods provide for an upper boundary for estimates of tax evasion or the shadow economy.

Analyzing the data using the different approaches at different points in time reveals interesting characteristics of the data that might be used in an estimate of the "unmeasurable". Moreover, it is most important for policymakers and scientists alike that they can find out which variables have an impact on tax evasion, tax morale, the shadow economy and undeclared work, whatever it is that is measured, and whatever method is used. If a set of policy instruments has consistent influences across tax compliance measures, the confidence in their use to achieve certain policy goals is substantially increased. This is the reason why experimental methods are a very important research tool in the analysis of tax compliance. Although it is the size of the shadow economy, of tax evasion or of undeclared work which attracts such enormous attention from the media and from policymakers, this is less important than the knowledge of which factors influence tax compliance in what directions.

2.4 The Method of Choice in this Study

In this report, we choose to measure undeclared work by the direct survey method not because we think it is a superior method of measuring undeclared work, but because using this approach allows us to focus strongly on undeclared earnings as defined above as distinct from both illegal activities and from capital income tax evasion and other kinds of tax evasion at full market price, where only one side benefits. It is thus possible to focus on compliance behavior in the labor market. Moreover, the survey method provides the possibility of getting detailed information on the environmental conditions for undeclared work. A major disadvantage of the macroeconomic indirect methods lies in the fact that central variables of the economic analysis of crime, namely the probability of detection and the fines, are almost always left out of the analysis. This is corrected in our survey approach by directly asking people about their perception of the risk and the punishment that they would expect. Before we describe how we have designed the survey for this study in order to get detailed information and to minimize the disadvantages of the direct method, we present overviews of existing estimates of the size of the German shadow economy and some comments on deterrence policies in Germany.

Chapter 3
The Size of the German Shadow Economy and Tax Morale According to Various Methods and Definitions

Different estimates obtained with the methods described above are summarized in Tables 3.1, 3.2 and 3.3. In Table 3.1, we show estimates of the shadow economy measured relative to official GDP, rates of participation in undeclared work are shown in Table 3.2, tax morale in Table 3.3. The tables build on and extend Table 3.1 in Feld and Larsen (2005, p. 32) and Table 12 in Feld and Schneider (2010, p. 132), and we add own estimates which have not been published before. The tables cover the period 1970 up to and including 2007. As the definitions used differ, estimates presented in the same table may not be directly comparable.

If we look at the estimates produced by the various methods, different patterns emerge. The employment gap method (Table 3.2) and the transactions approach (Table 3.1) seem to show the upper limit of the size of the German shadow economy measured either by the participation rate or relative to official GDP. The employment gap figures indicate the share of the labor force that works in the shadow economy but the figures do not reveal anything about their contribution to unofficial GDP. They are not directly comparable with any of the other estimates. As far as the figures produced by the transactions approach are concerned, a size of the shadow economy of one third of the official economy in the middle of the eighties seems unlikely, given that according to nearly all other estimates, the shadow economy grew further in the nineties.

The figures from the income gap method for the 1970s are significantly lower than those produced by the transactions approach, but mostly larger than those from the currency demand and the hidden (latent) variable approaches (Table 3.1). This may indeed be reasonable, because the income gap method supposedly includes capital income tax evasion, so that it should produce a higher figure than measures that mainly focus on labor income. This qualitative evidence for Germany is corroborated to some extent by evidence from the U.S. and Switzerland. A comparison of the estimates of the extent of tax evasion produced by the auditing approach of the IRS (Engel and Hines 1999) with the size of the shadow economy reported by Schneider and Enste (2000) using the currency demand approach shows that the former produces the largest estimates. Although based on a micro-approach, it also uses an income gap measure. Similarly, a comparison of the extent

L.P. Feld and C. Larsen, *Undeclared Work, Deterrence and Social Norms*,
DOI 10.1007/978-3-540-87401-0_3,

Table 3.1 The size of the shadow economy and the extent of undeclared work in Germany (relative to official GDP) according to different methods and definitions

Methods	1970	1975	1980	1985	1990	1995	2000	2001	2002	2003	2004	2005	2006	2007
Survey														
IfD Allensbach (1975)	–	3.6	–	–	–	–	–	–	–	–	–	–	–	–
Feld and Larsen (2012)[a]	–	–	–	–	–	–	–	4.1	–	–	3.1	3.6	1.8	3.2
West Germany	–	–	–	–	–	–	–	4.1	–	–	2.8	3.2	1.8	2.8
East Germany	–	–	–	–	–	–	–	4.3	–	–	4.4	4.8	2.5	4.4
Enste et al. (2009)[b]	–	–	–	–	–	–	–	–	–	–	–	–	6–7	–
Income gap[c]														
Lippert and Walker (1997)	11.0	10.2	13.4	–	–	–	–	–	–	–	–	–	–	–
Physical input														
Schneider and Enste (2000)[d]	–	–	–	14.5	14.6	–	–	–	–	–	–	–	–	–
Transactions														
Schneider and Enste (2000)[e]	17.2	22.3	29.3	31.4	–	–	–	–	–	–	–	–	–	–
Currency demand														
Kirchgässner (1983)	3.1	6.0	10.3	–	–	–	–	–	–	–	–	–	–	–
Langfeldt (1984a, b)	12.1	11.8	12.6	–	–	–	–	–	–	–	–	–	–	–
Schneider and Enste (2000)[f]	4.5	7.8	9.2	11.3	11.8	12.5	14.7	–	–	–	–	–	–	–
Hidden variable[g]														
Frey and Weck-Hannemann (1984)	5.8	6.1	8.2	–	–	–	–	–	–	–	–	–	–	–
Pickhardt and Sardà Pons (2006)	–	–	9.4	10.1	11.4	15.1	16.3	–	–	–	–	–	–	–
Schneider (2010)	4.2	5.8	10.8	11.2	12.2	13.9	16.0	16.0	16.6	17.1	16.1	15.4	15.0	14.7
Soft modeling														
Weck (1983)	–	8.3	–	–	–	–	–	–	–	–	–	–	–	–

Sources: See front column of the table

1970–2000: Estimates are placed as close as possible to the year they concern. For example, the survey estimate 3.6% in 1975 is for 1974 and the currency demand estimate 14.7% in 2000 is for 1997/1998

[a]The shadow economy ("Schwarzarbeit") relative to official GDP calculated on the basis of hours worked by the 18–66-year-olds and the wages pertaining in the official economy. Two rounds of interviews in 2006 both resulted in extraordinarily low rates of participation in undeclared work. In Feld and Larsen (2008) p. 10, the most extreme of the two was excluded and therefore the estimate (2.5%) differs from the 1.8% in this table where we have chosen to include both in order to have enough observations to show the distribution by region. Data for 2007 have not been published before. Data for 2001 were first published in Pedersen (2003)

[b]The shadow economy ("Schwarzarbeit") relative to official GDP calculated on the basis of hours worked and the wages pertaining in the official economy. 18 years and older

[c]Discrepancy between expenditure and income

[d]Physical input: electricity consumption. Refer to work by Mariá Lackó

[e]Refer to work by Edgar L. Feige

[f]Refer to work by Vito Tanzi

[g](DY)MIMIC estimates, a combination of the currency demand approach and the Multiple Indicators Multiple Causes (MIMIC) method

Table 3.2 Participation in undeclared work in Germany, West/East Germans admitting that they had carried out undeclared work, in percent

Methods	1970	1975	1980	1997	1998	2001	2003	2004	2005	2006	2007
Survey											
Lamnek et al. (2000)[a]	–	–	–	29/16	–	–	–	–	–	–	–
Mummert and Schneider (2001)[b]	–	–	–	–	25/13	–	–	–	–	–	–
Schneider (2004b)[c]	–	–	–	–	–	–	25	–	–	–	–
Enste et al. (2009)[d]	–	–	–	–	–	–	–	–	–	21	–
Eurobarometer (2007)[e]	–	–	–	–	–	–	–	–	–	–	3–4
Feld and Larsen (2012)[f]	–	–	–	–	–	10/11	–	8/13	10/14	5/8	9/11
Employment gap[g]											
Langfeldt (1984a, b)	23	39	34	–	–	–	–	–	–	–	–

[a]18 years and older
[b]14 years and older. Proportion of the interviewed which has ever carried out undeclared work
[c]Works regularly in the shadow economy
[d]18 years and older. Period: 2006
[e]15 years and older. Period: the last 12 months. Results are reported separately for two types of undeclared work. If there is no overlap between the two, the maximum rate of participation is 4% among East Germans as well as among West Germans. "In view of the sensitivity of the subject, the pilot nature of the survey and the low number of respondents who reported having carried out undeclared work or having received 'envelope wages', results should be interpreted with great care" (Special Eurobarometer 284/Wave 67.3, p. 3)
[f]18–74 years. Period: the last 12 months. Two rounds of interviews in 2006 both resulted in extraordinarily low rates of participation in undeclared work. The figures for 2006 and 2007 have not been published before. Data for 2001 were first published in Pedersen (2003)
[g]Discrepancy between official employment and actual employment according to other sources indicates the share of the labor force working in the shadow economy
Sources: See front column of the table

Table 3.3 Tax morale in Germany. Respondents replying that tax evasion is not acceptable at all, in percent

Method	1981	1990	1997	1999	2004	2005	2006	2007
Survey								
WVS/EVS (2009)[a]	–	51	47	57	–	–	57	–
West Germany[b]	52	40	40	57	–	–	47	–
East Germany[b]	–	67	54	59	–	–	67	–
Eurobarometer (2007)[c]	–	–	–	–	–	–	–	53
West Germany	–	–	–	–	–	–	–	53
East Germany	–	–	–	–	–	–	–	50
Feld and Larsen (2012)[d]	–	–	–	–	46	44	51	46
West Germany	–	–	–	–	44	42	49	45
East Germany	–	–	–	–	52	54	57	54

Answered 1 on a scale from 1 to 10, where 10 = totally unacceptable
[a]18 years and older
[b]Own calculations based on data available online at www.worldvaluessurvey.org. The exact actual values may differ to some extent from these figures
[c]15 years and older
[d]18–74 years. With the exception of a total for 2004 (Feld and Larsen 2005) these results are published for the first time in this book
Sources: WVS/EVS (2009) The World and European Values Surveys; Eurobarometer (2007); Feld and Larsen (2012); The Rockwool Foundation Research Unit's Shadow Economy surveys

of tax evasion according to the income gap and the shadow economy according to currency demand for Switzerland shows higher figures when using the income gap method (Feld and Frey 2005).

Table 3.1 also shows that according to the physical input method, the size of the shadow economy relative to GDP amounted to 14.6% in 1990 which is somewhat higher than figures from the currency demand and the hidden variable approaches. In the mid-1970s, the soft modeling approach produced an estimate of 8.3% which was higher than all but one unusually high estimate from the currency demand and the hidden variable approaches but lower than the estimates from the income gap and the transactions approaches.

Independent of which authors have conducted the analysis, the currency demand figures and those obtained from the hidden variable approach are relatively close together and in most cases slightly lower than those from the income gap method. The currency demand estimates by Langfeldt (1984a, b) is an exception to that rule. Otherwise the largest deviations are of the order of 2–3% points. The closeness of the outcomes of using these two methods is not really surprising, given the fact that the estimates from the hidden variable approach are derived by taking point estimates from the currency demand approach. Both approaches show an increase in the size of the shadow economy during the 1980s and 1990s. Only recently, since 2004, do the estimates by Schneider (2010) show a slight decline. It thus appears to be more realistic that these methods provide the upper boundaries of hidden activities, whereas the survey estimates in Table 3.1 of the extent of undeclared work relative to official GDP clearly provide the lower boundaries.

The survey figures in Table 3.2 regarding the rate of participation in undeclared work do not give a uniform picture. The results reported by Lamnek et al. (2000) for 1997, by Mummert and Schneider (2001) for 1998, Schneider (2004b) for 2003, Enste et al. (2009) for 2006 and Eurobarometer (2007) for 2006–2007 can be compared to those presented in the following chapters of this book. However, as it appears from the notes to Table 3.2, the surveys differ in various ways with regard to sampling, how far back in time the questions go, definitions, survey design and the way questions are formulated.

The studies by Lamnek et al. (2000) for 1997 and by Mummert and Schneider (2001) for 1998 found considerable differences between West and East Germany, while we did not find any significant differences for 2001. This changed as from 2004, but with the opposite sign, as the participation rate begins to increase in East Germany, a development which also manifests itself in the extent of undeclared work measured relative to GDP in Table 3.1.

Moreover, the proportion of respondents conceding that they had carried out undeclared work differs significantly from survey to survey. This is at least in part due to the way the questions where asked. Mummert and Schneider (2001), for example, report the proportion that had ever carried out undeclared work, whereas we report the proportion that had done it within the last 12 months. On the other hand, Enste et al. (2009) also ask about undeclared work within the last 12 months, while 25% of the respondents in Schneider (2004b) said that they did it on a regular basis. It is beyond the scope of this chapter to go deeper into the differences from survey to survey which may explain the different outcomes. The relatively narrow definition of "Schwarzarbeit" and the design of the Rockwool Foundation Research Unit's shadow economy surveys are described in detail in Chap. 5.

As already mentioned in the notes to Tables 3.1 and 3.2, the outcomes for 2006 in this study and Eurobarometer (2007) have been affected by one or more of the particular flaws and risks which the survey approach suffers from: some questions may not work, the questionnaire design may not be sufficiently well adapted to the context it is used in, the interviewers and/or the respondents may not understand the questions, the respondents may not want to answer them or may not answer honestly, external events may influence the interview situation, something may go wrong with the sampling of respondents. We have chosen to show the results from both of the surveys carried out in 2006 in the following chapters in spite of the extraordinarily low rate of participation in especially one of them, but the results can only be considered tentative and must be interpreted with extra great care. However, although the extent of undeclared work cannot be inferred based on the surveys just mentioned, these interviews may still give valuable information about the structure of the labor market where undeclared work takes place.

Even though the results do not lead to any clear-cut conclusions, survey estimates providing the lower boundaries of undeclared work as well as the hidden variable estimates providing the upper boundaries at least seem to indicate that hidden activities did not increase from 2004 to 2007. However, based on the information available in Tables 3.1 and 3.2, it also appears that during the years immediately before the period, undeclared work increased in East Germany and decreased in West and then settled at these new levels.

Table 3.3 shows the share of respondents replying that tax evasion is not acceptable at all (1 on a scale from 1 to 10). The WVS (World Values Survey), the Rockwool Foundation Research Unit's shadow economy surveys (Feld and Larsen 2012) and Eurobarometer (2007) all include such a question to assess tax morale. Differences in framing of the question may influence the answers, but the outcomes may to a large degree be considered comparable.

What is evident from the table is that tax morale declined considerably in West Germany during the 1980s, by more than 20%. Tax morale increased considerably from the mid- until the end of the 1990s. Data for East Germany are not available until 1990 and indicate that tax morale decreased from 1990 to 1999, but from a very high level. Thus, in 1999, tax morale was practically identical in West and East Germany where 57% and 59% respectively replied that it can never be justified to cheat on taxes if one gets the chance to do so. This is well in line with the surveys of the extent of and participation in undeclared work carried out in 2001 (Feld and Larsen 2012), but not with Lamnek et al. (2000) or Mummert and Schneider (2001). However, only 2 years before, in 1997, answers would be much more in line with the latter two studies, so it is a rather dramatic change in tax morale from 1997 to 1999. This descriptive evidence is somewhat corroborated by the estimation results of Feld et al. (2009)

Overall, tax morale appears not to have changed from 1999 to 2006, but actually it increased by 8 percentage points in East and decreased by 10 percentage points in

West Germany. This is not consistent with actual behavior by region according to Tables 3.1 and 3.2, but if one only looks at the totals, the net result is that neither tax morale nor undeclared work seem to have increased from 1999 to 2006. Our own assessments in this book only cover the period 2004–2007 but the picture is the same as in the WVS: tax morale apparently is higher in East Germany than in West Germany. The share of respondents saying that tax evasion is totally unacceptable is not quite as high as in the WVS, but that may be due to different framing in the two survey designs. The estimate from Eurobarometer (2007) for Germany as a whole is 51 compared with 57 and 46, but the Eurobarometer survey differs from the other results in the sense that tax morale is about the same in East Germany as in West Germany, even slightly, but not significantly, higher in West than in East.

Based on the hidden variable estimates by Schneider (2010) reported in Table 3.1, the increasing tax morale by the turn of the millennium does not appear to immediately translate into a smaller amount of undeclared work, but from an overall perspective it actually may have done so after a time lag, as might be cautiously guessed from the slight decline in the shadow economy suggested by Schneider's (2010) recent estimates. Such a development should be regarded positively. When we introduce the regional dimension it obscures the picture somewhat. The survey evidence reported in this study could shed additional light on developments across time.

Chapter 4
Deterrence in Germany: A Primer

If the theoretical models are correct, a reduction in the size of the shadow economy, if it indicates a trend reversal, could be the result of increased deterrence, tax or social policy reforms, or additional pressure from social norms. As the last of these develops slowly over time and is influenced by more important institutional changes, such as a shift in the tax authorities' treatment of taxpayers (Feld and Frey 2002b) or the introduction of direct democracy (Weck-Hannemann and Pommerehne 1989), we leave this possible explanation aside for the moment. We will focus first on changes in deterrence. This is, however, rather difficult to do, because the administration of the German tax system is not uniform across the country, due both to German administrative federalism, i.e., the strong role that the state administrations have in auditing and tax investigations, and to the differences in the sentences imposed by the courts in different states.

4.1 Punishing Tax Cheating by Fines and Imprisonment

In a recent paper, Feld et al. (2011) give an overview of deterrence measures to fight tax evasion and undeclared work in Germany. The main results of their analysis are summarized here. The legal foundation of the prosecution of tax evasion, which is always present with undeclared work, is the general fiscal code (AO). Additionally, if not otherwise stated in the relevant tax laws, the general criminal code (StGB), the code of criminal procedure (StPO) and the regulatory offences act (OWiG) apply. Below this level of statute law, the administrative instructions issued to the criminal departments and the case law based on the decisions of the Federal Finance Court (which functions as appellate court) are all of importance. According to AO §370, tax evasion is committed through misrepresentation to tax authorities or concealment of information relevant for taxation, through neglect of tax disclosure duties, or through failure to use compulsory tax stamps.

Possible punishments for tax evasion range from a fine to a prison sentence up to 5 years. In serious cases of tax evasion in combination with the abuse of official

L.P. Feld and C. Larsen, *Undeclared Work, Deterrence and Social Norms*,

DOI 10.1007/978-3-540-87401-0_4, © Springer-Verlag Berlin Heidelberg 2012

authority or with fraud, the possible sentences range from a minimum of 6 months up to a maximum of 10 years of imprisonment. Thc fines depend on the amount of taxes evaded, cooperation in the proceedings, and the individual daily net income of the tax evader. Fines start at the equivalent of six times the daily net income and can be up to 360 times the daily net income (with the accountable part of daily net income ranging from €1 to €5,000). Regional Tax Offices (OFD) have developed sentence tables for standard cases of tax evasion. Six examples of mild (Magdeburg and Stuttgart), average (Chemnitz and Muenchen) and severe (Berlin and Saarbruecken) sentencing are shown in Fig. 4.1. The large regional differences result from the high degree of autonomy of the regional tax offices. In 2008, the Bundesgerichtshof which is the highest federal court below the federal constitutional court decided to establish minimum sentences for particular severities of tax evasion. Tax evasion of €100,000 and above must be punished by prison sentences. In very severe cases of more than one million Euros concealed taxes, no agreement between the state and the taxpayers outside the court can be concluded anymore.

The main offence within the category of tax misdemeanors (i.e. minor offences against tax laws) could be literally translated as "tax shortening" (§378 Leichtfertige Steuerverkürzung). In comparison to tax evasion, "tax shortening" is not the result of a deliberate act, but of gross negligence. Gross negligence is presumed if, for example, the taxpayer does not hand in a tax return, does not inform himself about his tax duties, or does not scrutinize the tax statement prepared by his tax advisor.

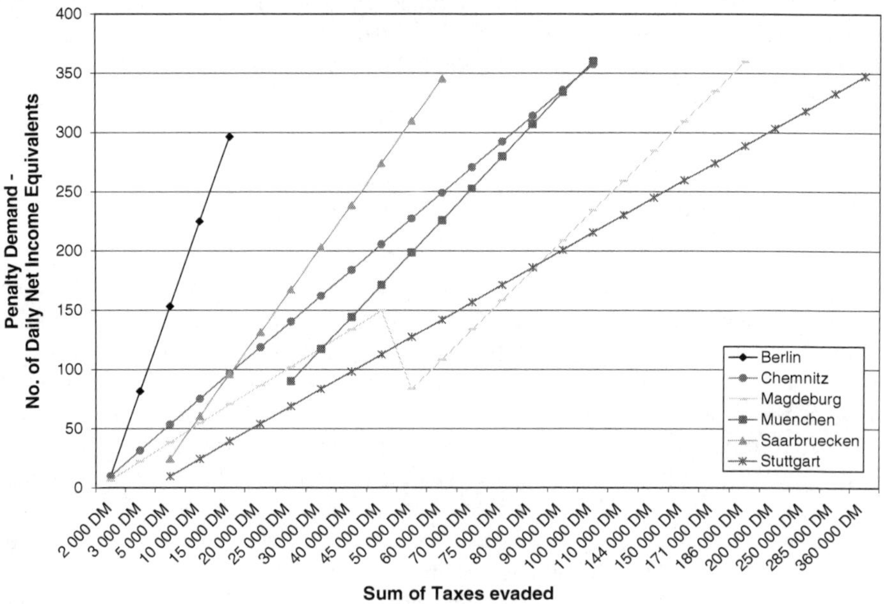

Fig. 4.1 Penalties requested for tax evasion. Administrative instruction tables of different regional tax offices (Source: INF. Informationen für Steuern und Wirtschaft, 1998, 11, pp. V, Feld et al. (2011))

"Tax shortening" can also be an offence by tax advisors or accountants if they do not pay necessary professional attention. In contrast to the Anglo-American system, tax misdemeanors can only be punished by fines in Germany. For "tax shortening" a fine of up to €50,000 can be imposed.

The German general criminal tax code has remained relatively unchanged after 1969. Apart from editorial revisions, only three changes since seem to be relevant. First, in 1993, taxes and customs duties of the European Union (EU) fiscal code became taxes in the sense of the German criminal tax code. Second, in 2001, the maximum fine for evasion of withholding taxes was increased from €5,000 to €25,000. Third, in 2002 the possibility of handing in amended returns was extended to tax evasion committed by accountants and in relation to organized crime (StGB § 370a). This change is intended to support whistle-blowing in criminal organizations. A person handing in an amended return can only be sentenced to half of the usual sentence. For the period 1982–2002 the developments in case law due to decisions of the Finance Courts, especially the BFH, are listed in Bilsdorfer (2003).

If we consider the developments in long time-series in the overall number of sentences and fines imposed for tax evasion in criminal proceedings (Fig. 4.2), i.e. the number of cases that were actually prosecuted, we see that the figures show peaks in severe punishment at the beginning of the 1980s as well as in the middle and late 1990s. The changes in the 1990s mainly result from offences in VAT, customs and excise duties, as the number of prison sentences and fines in criminal proceedings for other kinds of tax evasion stagnated (Fig. 4.3), and thus simply reflect the change in the law in 1993. With regard to the punishment of minor and major offences, it seems evident that the number of cases with fines for minor tax

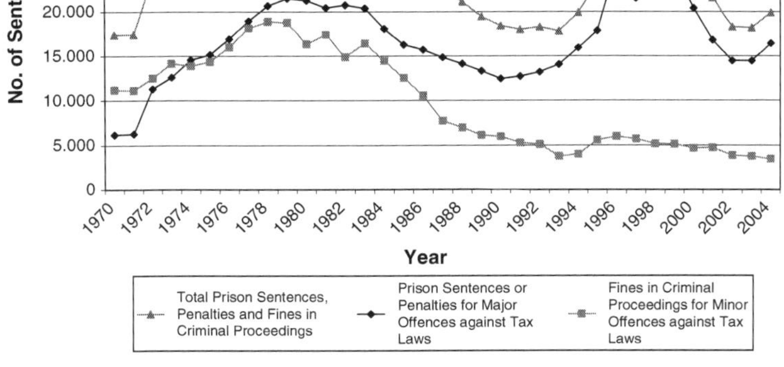

Fig. 4.2 Number of sentences and fines in criminal proceedings for tax evasion (Source: German tax offences statistics, BMF (1970–2005) (Feld et al. 2011))

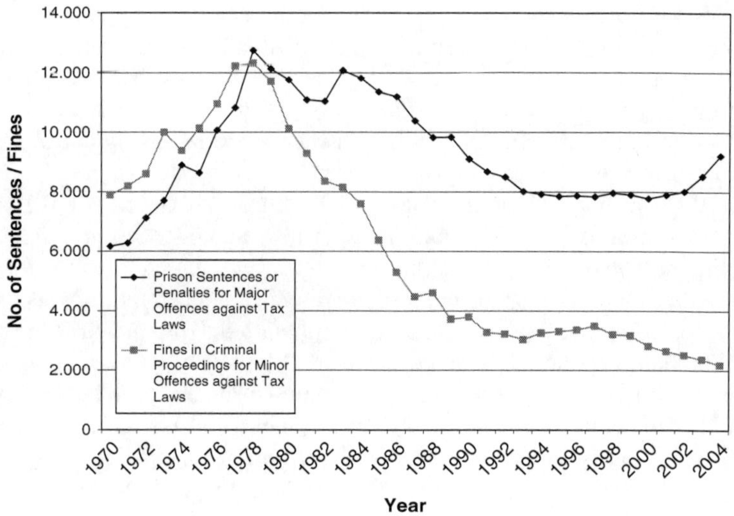

Fig. 4.3 Number of prison sentences and fines in criminal proceedings for tax evasion (Source: German tax offences statistics, BMF (1970–2005) (Feld et al. 2011))

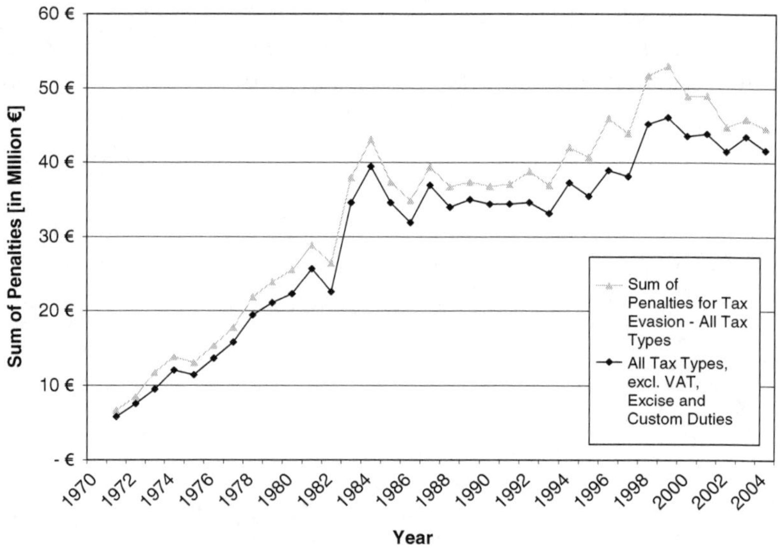

Fig. 4.4 Sum of penalties imposed for tax evasion, million Euros (Source: German tax offences statistics, BMF (1970–2005) (Feld et al. 2011))

offences decreased a lot more than the number of those with prison sentences or penalties for major tax offences.

Figures 4.4 and 4.5 indicate that these offences have been more severely punished since the middle of the eighties. For the sum of penalties imposed for

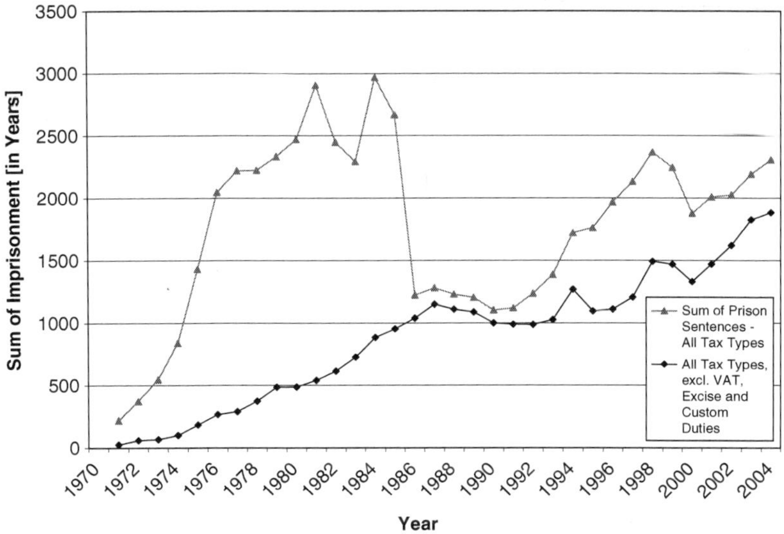

Fig. 4.5 Sum of prison sentences, years (Source: German tax offences statistics, BMF (1970–2005) (Feld et al. 2011))

tax evasion (Fig. 4.4) a steadily increasing trend can be observed since the beginning of the 1970s. For the sum of prison sentences (Fig. 4.5), i.e. in more serious cases of tax evasion, there is a decline which is first observable in the beginning of the 1980s and which became steeper during the end of the 1980s. When offences in cases of indirect taxation are excluded, the figures show a steady increase. This could, of course, simply reflect the fact that the extent of tax evasion and undeclared work has increased over time as well. But taking these figures together with those shown in Figs. 4.2 and 4.3, it can be seen that the lower number of offences which received prison sentences and fines were more heavily punished in terms of the amount of fines and the number of years in prison. Deterrence as measured by punishment has thus increased in Germany.

4.2 Deterring Tax Cheating by Auditing and Tax Inspections

In contrast to punishment, the intensity of control cannot easily be inferred from the statistics. As the German states are responsible for tax collection, they can use this competence in order to enter into a tax enforcement competition. In the German type of federalism, tax rates and tax bases are harmonized, and the only instrument left for tax competition is the frequency of tax auditing. Nevertheless, some figures are available. Figure 4.6 contains information on the average number of firms per auditor. The figures reveal that tax auditors have had to audit more and more firms on average since the beginning of the 1990s. This results in a decreasing

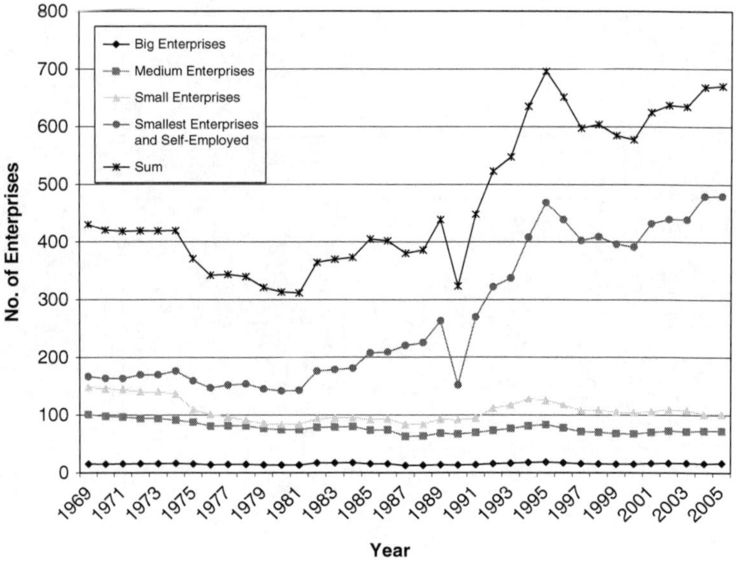

Fig. 4.6 Audit capabilities (on-site-inspections) 1969–2005, average number of firms per auditor (Source: Annual report about tax auditing in companies, BMF (1969–2005) (Feld et al. 2011))

probability of detection. However, this trend stopped at the end of the 1990s, due to the allocation of more and more customs officials to the investigation of undeclared work.

Taking the two variables punishment and audit capabilities together, it becomes obvious that deterrence as the product of these two variables generally increased from the mid-1990s until recently in Germany. If anything, an impact of deterrence on undeclared work could therefore be expected for that time period in particular. An empirical investigation comparing undeclared work across time is thus warranted.

4.3 A Uniform Framework to Deter Tax Cheating Since 2004

Since 2004, the *"Black Activities' Act"* provides for a uniform framework to investigate and sanction undeclared work and the shadow economy. It linked several different legal aspects of undeclared work from tax laws regarding tax evasion and fraud to social security or social assistance regarding social benefit fraud. Moreover, it entailed higher levels of deterrence by establishing the federal financial investigation unit (Finanzkontrolle Schwarzarbeit FKS) giving the federal government responsibility in a field that was mainly the task of the Länder (states) up to then. The FKS is part of the customs.

The FKS informs about its activities yearly. The statistics since 2005 are presented in Table 4.1. It reveals an increased intensity of control at the individual

Table 4.1 Results of the work of the federal financial investigation unit (Finanzkontrolle Schwarzarbeit FKS), 2005–2008

	2005	2006	2007	2008
Controls of individuals at the workplace	355,876	423,175	477,035	488,996
Control of employers	78,316	83,258	62,256	46,058
Concluded investigations in criminal proceedings	81,290	91,820	117,441	106,960
Concluded investigations of misdemeanors	53,852	54,087	72,969	63,274
	Million Euros			
Sum of penalties	67.1	46.4	51.9	56.7
Sum of damages according to investigations in criminal proceedings by FKS	562.8[a]	603.6	561.8	549.7
Sum of damages according to investigations in criminal proceedings by tax investigators of the Länder induced by intelligence of the FKS[b]	–	–	37.0	39.1
Sum of fines	21.2	19.8	25.4	33.9
Sum of prison sentences in years	995	1,123	1,398	1,556

[a]37 million Euros of it by special commissions
[b]In 2005 and 2006 not separately recorded
Source: BMF (2009). Entwicklung der Bekämpfung der Schwarzarbeit und der illegalen Beschäftigung, 11. Bericht der Bundesregierung, Monatsbericht, September 2009, p. 68

level across time while the control of employers decreased considerably. The number of concluded investigations first increased until 2007 and then slightly decreased. Overall, the sum of penalties and fines in million Euros and the sum of prison sentences in years increased steadily indicating the considerable increase in deterrence the new law and the new investigation unit brought. The FKS mainly concentrates on professional forms of undeclared work, for example, in the construction sector where the phenomenon is not infrequently accompanied by illegal immigration. Thus, the statistics in Table 4.1 also give a flavor as to how widespread undeclared work is in Germany.

Chapter 5
Design of the Survey

5.1 Reasons for Choosing the Survey Method

Our empirical investigation is based on data on undeclared work collected in 12 surveys of individuals in Germany from April 2001 through March 2007. A survey is the only approach based on field data that allows the testing of the impact of deterrence on such activities, given the current state of research in this field in Germany. Due to the German tax secrecy laws, no individual data, e.g., data comparable to that collected in the U.S. Taxpayer Compliance Measurement Program (TCMP), are available from the fiscal authorities that would allow the analysis of that relationship. Moreover, aggregate data, at the German state level, for example, do not help to get any information on the influence of deterrence, because the state fiscal authorities do not provide satisfactory data on the size of fines and the intensity of control. In the survey approach, however, it is possible to ask respondents about their perception of the risk of being detected and of the size of fines, in addition to their undeclared work. This possibility of measuring deterrence and other not immediately observable factors like social norms is one of the most important advantages of the survey method as compared to the other methods used to measure the shadow economy.

Moreover, the survey method has the advantage of eliciting additional details on the structure of undeclared work. Most other methods developed to measure the shadow economy are unable to distinguish between the various elements it comprises (undeclared work under informal (non-observable) market conditions, non-declaration of earned income and sales under formal market conditions, illegal economic activities, non-declaration of capital or transfer income, etc.). It has therefore been important to inform the respondents that we are focusing on the part of the shadow economy which in Germany is known as *"Schwarzarbeit"* and to explain precisely which part: purchases and sales or exchanges of services and goods, where the buyer and seller agree not to declare the activity (fully) to the authorities and both (mostly) benefit in some way from this non-declaration. Normally because prices and wages paid are below the formal market price and

L.P. Feld and C. Larsen, *Undeclared Work, Deterrence and Social Norms*,
DOI 10.1007/978-3-540-87401-0_5,

the parties, so to speak, split the tax, VAT, and social security contributions saved between them. But the advantage to the buyer may also be, for example, quicker delivery of a piece of work that is in short supply at the formal market. The key is the mutual awareness and agreement between the buyer and the seller that the activity is not (fully) declared to the authorities. Furthermore, the method used here allows us to measure not only the activities where payment is in cash, but also those paid for in kind, or in the form of a quid pro quo, i.e. exchange of goods and services. As mentioned in Chap. 2, we use the term "undeclared work" in this sense.

As also mentioned in Chap. 2, the survey approach has its own particular flaws, like any other method. Respondents may not tell the truth or the whole truth, and there is always a certain amount of non-response which can give a distorted picture of the true extent of, in this case, undeclared work. This shortcoming can partly be overcome by a structured interview in which the interviewer can pay particular attention to the slightest indication that respondents are understating the true extent of their participation in undeclared work, e.g., by repeating the relevant questions, or by underlining that the survey is exclusively used for scientific purposes and does not involve any personal disadvantage for the respondent. The strategy of using a structured interview technique has indeed been followed in this study, but, nevertheless, it must be emphasized that the data produced by the survey method represent the lower limit of the estimate of the extent of undeclared work in Germany.

5.2 How to Measure Undeclared Work in the Survey

In this chapter, we describe how we have designed the survey in order to get as detailed information as possible and to minimize the disadvantages of the method. The basic design of the questionnaire and the formulation of most of the questions have been developed and thoroughly tested several times in a Danish context since 1980. However, when applying the Danish questionnaire to German conditions, the design of the questionnaire had to fulfill two additional criteria: the questions should be comparable to the Danish questionnaire in order to allow for cross-country comparisons, and they should take account of differences in fiscal legislation between the two countries.

Neither "undeclared work" nor "undeclared activities" are direct translations of the terms used in the Danish and German questionnaires. In these, and in questionnaires used in Norway and Sweden, country-specific terms which the general publics are familiar with were used, e.g. "sort arbejde" in Denmark and "Schwarzarbeit" in the German questionnaire.

Clear-cut examples of undeclared work are those where money is exchanged under the mutual understanding between buyer and seller that income taxes, social security contributions, and VAT are not paid. This keeps prices below the full market price and still allows both parties to benefit from the exchange. Bricklaying, carpentry, cleaning, day-care, hairdressing, and the selling of farm products are often seen as examples, but undeclared work is not restricted to certain areas or trades, and neither does the person performing the activity have to operate within his or her own trade. Finally, undeclared work does not necessarily involve in-cash transactions. In Danish legislation, it also includes the sale of goods and services where payment is in the form of a quid pro quo, whether rendered immediately or later, so-called reciprocal favors. Danish fiscal legislation does not distinguish between income in the form of money and income in the form of other economic benefits.

As an example of the latter, the official tax assessment manual (Ligningsvejledningen) for several years has mentioned a bricklayer who did some work for his brother-in-law, a mechanic (e.g. Skatteministeriet 2001, p. 95). In return, the brother-in-law worked on the bricklayer's car. The mechanic was taxed on the value of the bricklaying, while the bricklayer was taxed on the value of the car repairs. In these situations, the work must be taxed irrespective of whether it is within the line of work of the person(s) concerned, and irrespective of whether an asset of economic value has been created, but because a payment has been made for work carried out. Similarly, persons who help each other build their own homes are liable to pay tax according to the value of the work the others have done for them, carpenters and accountants alike. Fiscally, the Danish Inland Revenue regards family members outside the nuclear family as non-family members, which means that work done on the parents' house by a son still living at home will count as a do-it-yourself activity (DIY), while it will count as a taxable activity if he has moved from home, provided he receives something in return.

In practice, the Inland Revenue will not pursue many of the reciprocal favors which are in effect a quid pro quo. This may be the case if the asset or service is not of a certain significance, but since no lower triviality limit is defined by law, and since a quid pro quo, according to law, is taxable, such activities are included in the Danish measurement of undeclared work. Trivial things like doing a sick neighbor a favor by taking his dog for a walk are not included, even though the neighbor may be expected to return the favor some day. Neither are material services included where no payment or return of the service is expected. In such cases, the service may be regarded as a gift, on which the recipient may be liable to tax, but which is not regarded as undeclared work as far as the donor is concerned. To some extent, it will be up to the interviewers to decide whether an activity should be defined as undeclared work or not, and in the Danish, but not in the German surveys, a written instruction described the dividing line between undeclared work and reciprocal favors such as neighborhood help as follows:

> The concept is regarded more broadly here. It does not have to involve money. Work or services which are only (now or later) expected to be 'paid for' in kind, and which some people often just regard as good neighborliness, reciprocal favors, etc., are also considered as 'undeclared activities' in this survey. Such activities give people an economic benefit which should be taxed. Only services within the nuclear family and completely trivial services outside the family fall outside our definition of undeclared activities—e.g. walking a sick neighbor's dog. However, it is regarded as an 'undeclared' activity if, for example, a farmer permanently stables a horse for a neighbor, who, in return, drives the farmer's children to and from school every day.

Leaving the question of definition partly up to the interviewers involves a risk that it may vary among them. In addition to this, it cannot be ruled out that some interviewers may feel uncomfortable asking questions about undeclared work, i.e. about breaches of the law. In Denmark, Viby Mogensen et al. (1995) demonstrated an interviewer effect on the questions about undeclared work, i.e. whether the interviewer could inadvertently influence respondents' answers, not just by virtue of their appearance (gender, age, social status, possibly also skin color, etc.), but also through their own expectations and attitudes. An interviewer effect was also demonstrated on other sensitive questions. Using the highly qualified and experienced interviewers of Statistics Denmark and TNS Infratest Sozialforschung can, together with thorough training, diminish, but not totally eliminate these risks. Furthermore, it was decided to lead up to the sensitive questions by asking whether the respondents have carried out DIY work in the home—a related, but non-sensitive subject—and then continuing to the part about undeclared work with the following transition:

> The next questions are about what is popularly called 'undeclared work'. There is considerable evidence to show that a large part of the population accepts 'undeclared work' and 'undeclared trade in goods'—i.e. activities which circumvent the Inland Revenue, where all parties benefit because they do not pay tax or VAT, etc. This can involve 'undeclared activities' which you pay for in cash, but can also include reciprocal favors between friends, acquaintances and family members.

This is followed by the question itself:

> Have you carried out activities of this kind during the past year?

Before turning to the application of the Danish questionnaire to German conditions, it should be noted that the question refers to the previous 12 months and to the supply side, and that it is stressed again that all parties must benefit for an activity to be included.

The survey approach may also be sensitive to campaigns against undeclared work that are accompanied by intense media coverage, especially in the short term, as it will be difficult to separate an actual change in informal market behavior from a possible change in respondents' readiness to answer questions about it. The results of Danish surveys which were accidentally carried out immediately after, or at the same time as, raids or other peaks during the ongoing campaign accompanied by intense media coverage indicated that such a coincidence had a negative effect on respondents' readiness to answer (in the short term).

5.3 Adapting the Survey to Germany

In Germany, campaigns have been part of the strategy for some years. In his description of German legislation regarding undeclared work at the time of the Rockwool Foundation Research Unit's surveys in Germany in 2001, Pedersen (2003, p. 45) referred to the "Gesetz zur Bekämpfung der Schwarzarbeit", but stressed that "Schwarzarbeit" is not identical to what in this context is defined as undeclared work. This illustrates the variety of terms and definitions which are characteristic of this field of research. Basically, the "Gesetz zur Bekämpfung der Schwarzarbeit" states that work and services of any importance must not be carried out without informing the relevant authorities or without the necessary permits. Emphasis is not only on taxes and VAT, but equally on various social security contributions. Another feature is that buyer as well as seller can be fined (at that time: up to €300,000).

On June 27, 2002, new legislation ("Gesetz zur Erleichterung der Bekämpfung von illegaler Beschäftigung und Schwarzarbeit") was passed by the German Federal Council aiming particularly at the construction sector. Other features of the law are better exchange of information between authorities and heavier fines. The "Gesetz zur Intensivierung der Bekämpfung der Schwarzarbeit und damit zusammenhängender Steuerhinterziehung (SchwarzArbG)", which has already been referred to in Chap. 1, came into force on August 1, 2004. It is to be expected that these legislative initiatives, of which the latest coincided with the first of the two series of interviews carried out in August and October 2004, will have had a certain effect. However, no changes were made in the basic design of the questionnaire because of the changes in legislation between 2001 and 2004.

As mentioned in Chap. 1, until August 1, 2004, there was no clear definition of "Schwarzarbeit" in German fiscal legislation, but "all facts of importance to the tax authorities"—i.e. wages and fees, self-employed persons' incomes from running a business for profit, etc.—were to be reported regardless of the means of payment. With regard to any quid pro quo arrangement, in order for the transaction to be considered taxable, there must exist a binding agreement between the parties. The bricklayer and the mechanic in the example above, as well as the farmer and his neighbor and the house builders, are liable to pay taxes provided there is a binding agreement between the parties. They are liable to tax on the market value of the service or piece of work they receive.

Not included under taxable activities in Germany are most minor reciprocal favors, some of which would, in principle, be taxable in Denmark. Examples would be people helping each other to move house, or an elderly widow who allows a neighbor to use her garage in return for him looking after her garden. There is a grey area, however. Pedersen (2003, p. 47) mentions neighbors who help each other replace a few tiles on each other's roofs, which is not included under taxable activities. They may even replace all the tiles, but "if the activity has such a value that it would normally involve a binding agreement it would be taxable".

In consequence, in the German surveys, the introductory question about undeclared work has been divided into two parts, where the first part refers to payment in cash and the second to quid pro quos:

> Bei den nächsten Fragen geht es um das, was man allgemein 'Schwarzarbeit' nennt. Wir erheben diese Fragen im Auftrag einer Gruppe von unabhängigen dänischen Wissenschaftlern, die sich damit im Rahmen einer international vergleichenden Untersuchung befassen.
>
> Die dänischen Wissenschaftler verstehen unter 'Schwarzarbeit' das Folgende: Man arbeitet für jemanden anderen und ist sich dabei einig, dass das Entgelt nicht versteuert

> wird, obwohl man das eigentlich müsste. Beide Seiten kommen so etwas günstiger weg, weil dann keine Mehrwertsteuer anfällt und auch keine Einkommensteuer oder Beiträge zur Sozialversicherung zu zahlen sind. So etwas kommt häufig vor, zum Beispiel, wenn man für jemanden putzt oder Gartenarbeiten erledigt, beim Babysitten, beim Kellnern, bei Schreib- oder Programmierarbeiten. Auch beim Hausbau, beim Renovieren oder bei Autoreparaturen ist nicht versteuerte Arbeit weit verbreitet.
>
> Wie ist das bei Ihnen: Haben Sie selbst in den letzten 12 Monaten in dieser Form für jemand anderen gearbeitet?

As in the Danish question, the text emphasizes that the question is about undeclared work, work that has not been taxed even though it should have been, and that both parties must derive a benefit from this fact, whereas the part about the survey being carried out for a team of independent (Danish) researchers was added in the German questionnaire, because the results of the first pilot survey indicated a greater unwillingness to answer such a direct question about tax evasion. If the respondent still hesitated in answering, the interviewers were instructed to stress that all answers were treated in the strictest confidence. It was also stated that the data was being collected for the Rockwool Foundation Research Unit:

> Falls die Zielperson zögert, weisen Sie bitte nochmals auf die absolute Vertraulichkeit des Interviews hin. Die Angaben werden nur in anonymisierter Form und ausschließlich zu wissenschaftlichen Zwecken ausgewertet.
>
> Bei Nachfragen: Bei der dänischen Gruppe von Wissenschaftlern handelt es sich um die Forschungsgesellschaft der Rockwool-Stiftung in Kopenhagen—ein renommiertes unabhängiges Forschungsinstitut, das von dem Wirtschaftswissenschaftler Gunnar Viby Mogensen (as from 2004: Torben Tranæs) geleitet wird.

All respondents were then asked whether they had carried out undeclared work where payment had been in the form of a quid pro quo:

> Manchmal erfolgt die Bezahlung nicht bar, sondern in Form einer Gegenleistung. Das heißt, man arbeitet für jemanden und erwartet, dass der andere als Gegenleistung selbst etwas für einen tut.
>
> Haben Sie selbst in den letzten 12 Monaten solche Arbeiten durchgeführt, für die Sie von dem anderen eine Gegenleistung bereits bekommen haben oder noch erwarten?

As in the Danish question, the part about a quid pro quo stresses that respondents must either already have received a quid pro quo as payment or expect to do so in the future. The so-called "€400 Jobs" ("Geringfügige Beschäftigung" or "Minijobs") and "Midijobs", occupations with wages lower than €400 and €800 respectively with a special tax treatment, are not mentioned, as people in these jobs are not liable to pay tax on their wages, provided they stay within the specified limits, and it was assumed that respondents were able to make that distinction. However, in the most recent surveys a question was inserted which explicitly secures that a Minijob is not counted as undeclared work.

5.4 Conducting the Structured Interviews

As to the quality of the answers, the importance of highly qualified and experienced interviewers has already been mentioned. The private market research institute TNS Infratest Sozialforschung, which carried out the interviews in Germany, has extensive experience of collecting data for social science studies including, for example, for the "Sozio-ökonomische Panel"—SOEP (The German Socio-Economic Panel—GSOEP), a longitudinal data set which is widely used by researchers in Germany and abroad. While Computer Assisted Telephone Interviewing (CATI) is the method used by Statistics Denmark, it was decided to carry out the German interviews using Computer Assisted Personal Interviewing (CAPI). As telephone interviews are less costly to carry out than face-to-face interviews, and because telephone interviews had worked very well in previous Danish surveys, the same method was tested in a small-scale pilot survey in Germany, which was also intended to test the design of the questionnaire, before the actual survey. The data produced by the pilot survey, however, showed an unrealistically low frequency of undeclared work. It was, therefore, decided to carry out another pilot survey, this time by means of face-to-face interviews and using a revised design of the questionnaire. As the results of the second pilot survey as to the level and structure of undeclared work were closer to what was to be expected based on observations in other countries, the CAPI method and the question design above were chosen.

As in 2001, the questions in 2004–2007 were included in TNS Infratest Sozialforschung's face-to-face omnibus survey. As will emerge from the following, the samples were drawn at the household level, and to ensure a representative sample at the personal level, corrections were made using TNS Infratest Sozialforschung's standard weighting procedure for their face-to-face omnibus. And as in 2001, the first series of interviews carried out in 2004 served as a pretest. The purpose of the pretest in 2004 was partly to compare the level of undeclared work found with the results obtained in 2001, partly to check if changes and questions which were asked for the first time in 2004 caused problems during the field work. Field periods for the 12 waves of interviews are shown in Appendix Tables 5 and 6 which we will refer to in Chap. 6.

In Table 5.1, response rates and refusals for the surveys in 2001 and 2004–2007 are compared, and as can be seen, they are almost unchanged at levels of 64–66% and 16–17% respectively, which do not differ from the omnibuses in general. As can further be seen from Appendix Tables 1, 2, 3 and 4, the weighted distribution of respondents in the questionnaire surveys by gender, age, and region are reasonably representative of the population as a whole. The tables and figures in the following chapters are based on the 18–74-year-olds, and the number of interviews available with persons in this age group is shown in the last column of Table 5.1. In total, 1,096 observations were thus available for use in the empirical analysis in 2007, 2,176 in 2006, 2,144 in 2005, 2,143 in 2004, and 5,686 in 2001.

As will be shown in the first table of Chap. 6, the non-response (or so-called "item non-response", i.e. "don't know", "refusals", and "not stated") in the first question about having participated in undeclared work, which was 2.8% in 2001, decreased to only 1.3% in 2004, 0.7% in 2005, 0.8% in 2006, and 1.1% in 2007. This is remarkable, as questions related to income show much higher item non-response, due to the fact that income is traditionally sensitive information, and apparently even more sensitive than questions about undeclared work.

Table 5.1 Response and non-response rates, Germany, 2001 and 2004–2007

	Gross sample	Interviews available for analysis		Refusals		Interview method	Population	Interviews available with persons aged 18–74
	No.	No.	%	No.	%			
2001	9,706	6,396	65.9	1,670[a]	17.2	Face-to-face	14+	5,686
2004	3,856	2,532	65.7	633[b]	16.4	Face-to-face	14+	2,143
2005	3,860	2,480	64.2	672[c]	17.4	Face-to-face	14+	2,144
2006	3,846	2,535	65.9	626[d]	16.3	Face-to-face	14+	2,176
2007	1,933	1,267	65.5	316[e]	16.3	Face-to-face	14+	1,096

Source: The Rockwool Foundation Research Unit's Shadow Economy Surveys

[a]Of the 1,670 refusals, 798 mentioned lack of time as the reason for not participating in the interview

[b]Of the 633 refusals, 281 mentioned lack of time as the reason for not participating in the interview

[c]Of the 672 refusals, 318 mentioned lack of time as the reason for not participating in the interview

[d]Of the 626 refusals, 285 mentioned lack of time as the reason for not participating in the interview

[e]Of the 316 refusals, 137 mentioned lack of time as the reason for not participating in the interview

The level of undeclared work found in the Danish questionnaire surveys since 1980—and thus the reliability of the answers to questions about undeclared work—may be said to be supported by the estimates of unreported personal income mentioned in Chap. 2 resulting from examining discrepancies between Danish national accounts and tax statistics (Larsen 2002; Viby Mogensen 2003, and time series continued by the Danish Tax and Customs Administration). These estimates are based on a method used by the Danish Economic Council in the 1960s and 1970s to estimate tax evasion by comparing total personal incomes according to tax statistics with total personal net incomes derived from the national accounts statistics. Unfortunately, a similar possibility of comparing the results of our German surveys with results obtained by an alternative method, which measures approximately the same part of the shadow economy as we do, does not exist.

Chapter 6
The Incidence of Undeclared Work in Germany 2001–2007

6.1 The Proportion of the Population Engaged in Undeclared Work

It should be recalled that undeclared work in our surveys consisted of two components: someone is working for somebody else (1) for payment in cash or (2) for payment in kind or in the form of a quid pro quo or return service in order to save tax payments, VAT, and social security contributions and both parties in the transaction are aware of that.

Turning to the results of the interviews, Table 6.1 shows that, in 2001, the proportion of the population in the 18–74 age group (inclusive) who stated that they had carried out undeclared work ("Schwarzarbeit") within the last 12 months was 10.4%, which is the average of five waves of interviews. This share decreased to 8.8% in 2004 only to increase again to 11.1% the year after and then decrease to a comparatively low level of 5.8% in 2006. In 2007, one wave with about 1,100 interviews resulted in a participation rate of 9.7%.

It thus looks as if the participation rate varies around an average which would be almost exactly one in ten had it not been for the interviews in 2006 which pull the average down. Obviously, the low average of 5.8% in 2006 differs significantly from the general picture. The average participation rate is low according to both waves in 2006, but it is particularly low—4.5%—in the interviews carried out in October. Participation rates and field periods of each of the 12 waves of interviews during the period 2001–2007 are shown in Appendix Table 5.

According to the figures presented in Appendix Table 5, the average participation rate (10.7%) which results from interviews carried out from March through June is 1 percentage point higher than the average participation rate (9.7%) resulting from interviews carried out from August through October (the two waves in September–October 2006 not included). Whether the interviews were carried out during the first or during the last 6 months of the year thus does not appear to explain the difference between 2006 and the rest of the years. Furthermore, seasonal fluctuations in the results would point to a methodological problem

L.P. Feld and C. Larsen, *Undeclared Work, Deterrence and Social Norms*,
DOI 10.1007/978-3-540-87401-0_6,

Table 6.1 Proportion of the population in the 18–74 age group who has carried out undeclared work within the last year, Germany, 2001 and 2004–2007

	Carried out undeclared work?				
	Yes	No	Don't know/refusal	Total	Number of persons
	%	%	%	%	
2001	10.4	86.7	2.8	100	5,686
2004	8.8	89.9	1.3	100	2,143
2005	11.1	88.1	0.7	100	2,144
2006	5.8	93.4	0.8	100	2,176
2007	9.7	89.3	1.1	100	1,096

Source: The Rockwool Foundation Research Unit's Shadow Economy Surveys
Note: The sample has been drawn at the household level, and a weight has been applied to make the sample representative as to gender and age distribution and other characteristics of the total population

with the design of the questionnaire: i.e. that the average time horizon of the respondents is shorter than the last 12 months which the questions refer to in order to take into account that undeclared activities may not be evenly distributed over the year.

Finally, Table 6.1 also shows that the proportion of the respondents who could not or who refused to answer the question decreased from 2.8% in 2001 to just around 1% in 2004–2007.

The gender structure is shown in Table 6.2: the proportion of the population who had carried out undeclared work was quite steady between 13.4% and 15.8% among men except for the 7.8% in 2006. The participation rate among women generally was much lower and varied between 3.8% and 8.5% but apparently with a downward trend.[1]

Looking at the age structure of participants, a remarkable stability seems to be characteristic of the 30–39-year-olds and the 40–49-year-olds at levels around 12–13% and 9–11% respectively, when 2006 is disregarded. At the beginning of the period, the highest participation rates are found in the youngest age groups, but while the participation rate among the 18–19-year-olds increased by almost 50% from 2001 to 2004 and then decreased to a lower level in 2005 than in 2001, the participation rate among the 20–29-year-olds first decreased and then increased again. In 2006 as well as in 2007, the level among the 18–29-year-olds had decreased to about the same level as among the 30–39-year-olds and to an even lower level among the 18–19-year-olds. Already at the age of 30 average participation rates are beginning to decrease and are decreasing steadily with age. So the lowest rates – 1–3% – are found among the 70–74-year-olds. It is too early to conclude on the basis of one wave of interviews in 2007 that the decrease by age has been postponed and now sets in at the age of 40.

[1] Participation rates among men and women separately and in total in each of the 12 waves of interviews are shown in *Appendix Table 5*.

Table 6.2 Proportion of the population in the 18–74 age group who has carried out undeclared work within the last year, by gender, age and occupation, Germany, 2001 and 2004–2007

	Carried out undeclared work				
	2001	2004	2005	2006	2007
			%		
Men	14.5	13.4	13.9	7.8	15.8
Women	6.5	4.5	8.5	3.9	3.8
18–19-year-olds	16.6	24.3	13.9	5.4	9.7
20–29-year-olds	19.1	13.4	21.0	9.7	13.5
30–39-year-olds	13.2	12.2	13.3	8.1	13.3
40–49-year-olds	10.0	10.3	9.4	4.7	11.4
50–59-year-olds	7.4	5.1	8.5	6.2	9.2
60–69-year-olds	5.6	2.6	8.2	3.1	4.2
70–74-year-olds	1.0	3.0	2.9	1.3	2.4
Self-employed/assisting spouse	12.1	1.7	9.9	12.6	18.7
Salaried employees	7.1	8.9	10.2	4.0	10.2
Skilled workers	19.2	16.6	13.8	8.0	16.8
Unskilled workers	8.2	8.9	14.0	7.1	8.2
Unemployed	20.7	17.1	19.1	9.8	14.7
Pensioners	4.2	3.6	6.3	3.0	3.4
Students	27.3	14.6	15.3	6.7	14.9
Other	8.7	6.1	10.8	4.9	5.8
Total	10.4	8.8	11.1	5.8	9.7
Number of persons	5,686	2,143	2,144	2,176	1,096

Source: The Rockwool Foundation Research Unit's Shadow Economy Surveys
Note: The sample has been drawn at the household level, and a weight has been applied to make the sample representative as to gender and age distribution and other characteristics of the total population

It is an interesting age pattern that undeclared work among the 30–49-year-olds remained relatively constant across time, since the middle-aged people in Germany are those with the highest participation rate in legal working relations in the official labor market. As their participation rate in undeclared work remained relatively unchanged, the initial overall reduction from 2001 to 2004 and the subsequent resumption in 2005 have been driven mainly by people at the beginning or the end of their normal/official working lives, and by women, the exception being the 18–19-year-olds and the 70–74-year-olds, but obviously the divergent trends in these two age groups have not offset the general picture.

Table 6.2 also reveals an interesting pattern of undeclared work for the different occupations. The reduction from 2001 to 2004 was extremely marked among the self-employed/assisting spouses and students. However, the remarkable decrease from 12.1% to 1.7% for the self-employed/assisting spouses is unlikely to reflect solely an actual change in undeclared labor market behavior, despite the fact that the increase in deterrence in 2004 has been aimed mainly at this group. It rather points to the possibility mentioned earlier that respondents' readiness to answer questions about undeclared work may be affected temporarily by, e.g., ongoing campaigns aimed at reducing their participation in such activities. In 2005, the participation rate among the self-employed/assisting spouses was almost back at the same level as in 2001 and it increased further to 12.6% in 2006 and 18.7% in 2007. It is a notable development that the self-employed/assisting spouses – as the only occupational group – even experienced an increase from 2005 to 2006 and had the highest rate of all in 2007. The participation rate among students remained – again with 2006 as an exception – at the level around 15% which it had dropped to in 2004 from an exceptionally high level close to 30% in 2001.

The most important group when it comes to the number of persons involved in undeclared work, the skilled workers, reduced their participation from 2001 to 2004 and continued to do so in 2005 and 2006, but in 2007 this downward trend seems to have been reversed. In 2007, 16.8% of the skilled workers had carried out undeclared work within the last 12 months while it was 19.2% in 2001. Unskilled workers and pensioners remained relatively steady at 7–9% and 3–4% respectively, except for an isolated increase in both groups in 2005. Salaried employees and the unemployed also show relatively stable rates – at 7–10% and 15–21% respectively – but seemingly with a slightly upward trend as far as the salaried employees are concerned, while the unemployed seem to be moving in the opposite direction.

It is difficult to explain the exceptionally low figures found in the 2006 survey, especially in the data collected in October that year, as well as the uninterrupted increase among the self-employed and assisting spouses found in the last three surveys, which goes against the results for all other occupational groups. The participation rate is low both for men and for women in 2006, and the low level cannot be isolated to specific age groups or occupational groups.

It is obvious that these results must be interpreted with care and that an important question to investigate is how much is actually due to an apparently momentary drop in the level of participation in undeclared work in 2006 and how much is caused by other things. This must be kept in mind in the following, where we have decided to continue to include all of the data collected in 2006. We did so in spite of the ambiguous results and because we wanted to be able to include the data in our econometric analyses of characteristics which correlate with participation in undeclared work.

6.2 An Econometric Model to Explain Participation in Undeclared Work

To find out which variables have an impact on the probability of – or at least correlate with – participating in undeclared work, logistic regressions were subsequently performed. Logistic or probit regressions are the methods of choice whenever the dependent variable is a binary choice variable, i.e. when it can only take the values of 0 or 1. This is the case in this study, because participation in undeclared work is a dichotomous variable. The differences between logistic and probit regressions are not relevant for this study, in particular because the choice of the logistic regression method does not produce qualitatively different results from probit regressions. It should also be noted that the estimation results of logistic regressions (like those of probit regressions), i.e. the coefficient estimates, cannot easily be interpreted quantitatively due to the non-linear nature of the estimation procedure. Only relative interpretations are warranted. We therefore supplement the coefficient estimates with calculations of marginal effects which can be interpreted quantitatively.

The first step in the analysis is to include the socio-economic characteristics of the respondents. The impact of the important, theoretically based qualitative variables deterrence (perceived risk of detection and expected sanction), tax policy (perceived marginal tax), and social norms are gradually included in the analysis in the next chapters.

The results shown in Table 6.3 are from regressions performed separately for men and women. The regressions were performed separately primarily because the participation rate differs so significantly by gender and, as it turns out, the correlations found between explanatory variables and participating or not participating also to some extent are different for men and women. On the other hand, it turned out, as more variables were added as we do in subsequent chapters, that there is a trade-off between the wish to differentiate and the need to have sufficiently large data sets. We therefore made supplementary regressions where men and women are included at the same time in order to obtain larger data sets, and we will refer to the results of these regressions as well. Furthermore, we have made the same regressions including data from 2008, even though these data could not be fully integrated in this study. In Chaps. 8, 9 and 10, when qualitative variables are gradually added, further "sensitivity analyses" are made by looking at each year separately parallel with the regressions based on pooled data sets (2004–2007 and 2004–2008) and by dealing with the missing values in these new

Table 6.3 Logistic regression of the probability of participating in undeclared work, 18–74-year-olds, Germany, 2001 and 2004–2007

	Men	Women
Age	√	(√)
Marital status	–	√
Children under 6	–	–
Occupation	√	√
Education	√	(√)
Respondent's monthly net income	√	√
Length of unemployment	√	–
Region (East/West Germany)	–	–
Owner-occupied/not owner-occupied home	–	–
Year the survey was carried out	√	√

Source: The Rockwool Foundation Research Unit's Shadow Economy Surveys

Note: √: significant effect at least at the 5% level, (√): significant effect but only at the 10% level, –: not significant. Details are shown in Appendix Table 7. The sample has been drawn at the household level, and a weight has been applied to make the sample representative as to gender and age distribution and other characteristics of the total population

variables either by setting them to the median value of the answers given by other respondents or by considering missing as its own answer category.

The socio-economic variables included which may possibly influence the probability of participating in undeclared work are listed in Table 6.3: age, marital status, small children, occupation, education, income, unemployment, region, ownership of home. √ indicates that the variable has a significant impact in a logistic regression of the probability of participating in undeclared work with only socio-economic explanatory variables. Detailed regression results are shown in the appendix tables.

We use this first regression mainly to present the socio-economic variables we have chosen and their significance levels when they are all included at the same time, i.e. whether or not a particular variable has a statistically significant effect on the probability of having carried out undeclared work within the last year when all the other variables are also taken into consideration. We have pooled all our surveys from 2001 and 2004–2007 into one single data set and added a dummy variable for each year we have collected data. That allows us to examine whether or not the timing of the interview plays an independent role along with the socio-economic variables. The choice of variables is the same as in Pedersen (2003) who first presented the data from 2001. In later chapters we will compare the results in Pedersen (2003) directly with the results from 2004–2007.

From Table 6.3 and the details in Appendix Table 7, it can be concluded that as far as *age* is concerned, the probability of conducting undeclared work for men is higher for those younger than the reference group chosen (the 40–49-year-olds) and lower for those who are older. The effect is (highly) significant for the 18–29-year-olds and for the 60–74-year-olds. In the light of Table 6.2 above, this was to be expected, but it should be noted that for women, though the effect is only significant (at the 10% level) for the oldest age group, all other age groups than the 18–29-year-olds have a lower probability than the reference group. Overall, age thus has a negative effect on the probability of conducting undeclared work.

Marriage has a highly significant and negative effect for women, meaning that single women are more likely to carry out undeclared work than married women, while the variable is not significant for men when data from all the years are pooled. Having *small children* (under the age of 6) does not appear to be of any importance here.

Compared to the reference group (salaried workers), skilled men and women, unskilled women and female students have a significantly higher probability of being active on the undeclared labor market. Other *occupational groups* do not – in this model and all other things being equal – differ significantly from the salaried workers as far as their propensity to work undeclared is concerned. That skilled men and women differ significantly from the reference group is mainly driven by the data from 2001. If that survey is omitted, occupation is no longer significant. The high participation rate in this group was not as pronounced in some of the later surveys as it was in 2001 which was also the impression from Table 6.2.

In general, with respect to occupation and the other explanatory variables, there are (even marked) differences in the estimation results from year to year if we conduct the regressions for each year separately instead of pooling the data sets. This is also something that might be suspected from the descriptive data presented above and it can at least partly be attributed to the, after all, limited number of observations available in a single year's survey.

The most significant effect as far as *education* is concerned is that men who have completed Fachschule (secondary school) have a significantly higher probability of having carried out undeclared work within the previous 12 months than the reference group (beruflich-betriebliche Ausbildung, dual education).

Both men and women in the lowest *income* groups – the respondent has a monthly net income of up to €1,000 – have a higher probability of conducting undeclared work than the reference group which consists of respondents with the highest incomes (€2,000 per month or more). This effect is more significant for men than for women. Income has been grouped with approximately 20% of the respondents in each of the five groups. This effect can be ascribed also for a large part to 2001 and in various regressions based on pooled data sets – 2004–2007 as well as 2004–2008 and separate regressions for men and women as well as joint regressions – income is not significant. We will return to the differences between 2001 and later years in the next chapters when we have to omit 2001 because most of the questions behind the qualitative variables were not asked until 2004.

The longer a period of *unemployment* lasts, the higher the probability of undeclared work – for men. Finally, the *timing of the interviewing* also seems to play a role – for women. It was to be expected that 2006 would stand out as it does for both men and women, but with the strong reservations in mind we have aired about the results obtained that year, we will only point out other significant year dummies than 2006, i.e. 2004 and 2007, both in the regression for women and both negative compared with the reference year (2001). 2004 is only significant at the 10% level, however, whereas 2007 is highly significant which reflects the fact that the participation rate did not immediately return to the level it had the year before after the decrease in 2006 like it did for men. If we disregard 2006, this also corresponds to saying that the participation rate for men may very well have been the same each year.

Region and *home-ownership* are not significant in this specification of the model. In later chapters we will try other specifications and add the qualitative variables mentioned above. As mentioned, this means that we will have to perform many of the regressions without the data collected in 2001 because most of these variables were not included in the survey that year, but before doing so we will make comparisons of 2001 with 2004 and subsequent years which will be of interest because many of the initiatives against undeclared work took place from 2004 onwards.

6.3 Working Time Spent on Undeclared Activities

Respondents who had carried out undeclared work were asked to state the average time per week spent on such activities. First, answers from those respondents who could give an exact number of hours in the range 1–70 h (inclusive) were accepted and entered into the calculation of a weekly average for all 18–74-year-olds who had carried out such activities. Second, if the answer was not an exact number but, for example, "less than 1 h" or "don't know", the respondents were given the possibility of stating the total number of hours spent during the last 12 months instead. If this number of hours per year, divided by 52 and rounded off, resulted in a number of hours per week in the range 1–70 (inclusive), then that answer was entered into the calculation. Third, other respondents were assumed to spend an amount of time corresponding to the average for all participants.

On the one hand, it is a strong assumption to make that respondents who do report a weekly average in the range 1–70 h (inclusive) make up a representative sample of the whole group of people who say that they have done (some) work undeclared over the previous 12 months. It is quite likely that some people who answered yes to the question about undeclared work could not give a weekly average simply because they did not carry out such activities very often. Assuming that these people have spent as much time on undeclared work as the ones who actually reported time spent per week will bias the measure of the total number of hours spent in the undeclared sector of the economy upwards. On the other hand, the tax authorities' occasional raids show that there are people who work many hours – even full time – in the undeclared part of the economy, and it is to be expected that some of these people, if they are willing to report any undeclared work at all, will not be willing to report that they do it massively. They may not want to answer the question about weekly hours, but, if given the opportunity, may report some smaller number of hours worked during a whole year which lies within the limits of what is considered socially acceptable.

The extra piece of information obtained by asking a question about hours per year is likely to be unbiased with respect to those respondents who are only involved in undeclared activities occasionally, while for those who are heavily involved, it will lead to (further) underestimation. Allowing for this in the calculation of average time per week automatically increases any downward trend and curbs any upward trend in the level of undeclared work regardless of any real changes in the level. Not allowing for it, or doing so only partially, may be a way of allowing instead for the built-in shortcomings of the method that some respondents, in conflict with the truth, answer no to the question about involvement in undeclared work or deliberately underestimate the degree of involvement. In the latter case, it is implicitly assumed that the effect of underreporting at the very least offsets the fact that respondents doing undeclared work on a minor scale are entered into the calculations with a disproportionately large weight.

It was stressed to the interviewers that respondents who could not answer the question about average number of hours per week in the first place should be asked to reconsider the question, and that an estimate was better than no answer, before the alternative – the number of hours for a whole year – was mentioned. Still, including an alternative involves a risk that too little effort is made by the interviewer to get an answer to the first question, possibly resulting in an underestimation of the level, which must be weighed against the advantage of getting a higher response rate.

Table 6.4 Average time per week spent on undeclared work, 18–74-year-olds who have carried out undeclared work, Germany, 2001 and 2004–2007

	Average time per week spent on undeclared work	Proportion who specify time spent on undeclared work	Number of persons who have carried out undeclared work
	Hours:minutes	%	
2001	8:14	59.6	551
2004	7:30	49.9	182
2005	6:40	56.0	227
2006	6:25	58.3	131
2007	6:16	60.0	105

Source: The Rockwool Foundation Research Unit's Shadow Economy Surveys
Note: The sample has been drawn at the household level, and a weight has been applied to make the sample representative as to gender and age distribution and other characteristics of the total population. The number of persons shown in the table is the actual number before the weight was applied

The results are shown in Table 6.4, which indicates that the average time spent on undeclared activities was gradually reduced from 8¼ h in 2001 to 6¼ h in 2007, i.e. by 2 h or almost one fourth. About 60% of the respondents who had carried out undeclared work could also specify time spent on such activities during the last 12 months, the exception being the survey in 2004 where it was only reported by half of the respondents.

It was mentioned above and shown in Appendix Table 5 that the average participation rate is low according to both waves of interviews carried out in 2006, but particularly low in the interviews carried out in October of that year. In Table 6.4, 2006 does not stand out, but, like it was the case with the participation rate, average time per week spent on undeclared work according to the answers given in October 2006 is also the lowest in the 12 waves of interviews carried out during the period 2001–2007 (see Appendix Table 6). According to the figures presented in Appendix Table 6, the average time spent on undeclared activities by those who have carried out such activities, which results from interviews carried out from March through June, is approximately the same as in interviews carried out from August through October (the two waves in 2006 not included) – about 7½ h. This is in contrast to the participation rate which is somewhat (1 percentage point) *higher* in the interviews carried out in the first half-year than in the interviews carried out in the second half-year (the two waves in 2006 not included).

It is difficult to assess the importance of the information on average time spent on undeclared work per week. Given an official working week in Germany (which of course depends on the collective labor agreements in the different sectors) of say about 38 h, an undeclared working week in the interval 6¼ to 8¼ h amounts to 15–20% of that. It should be noted that this is the undeclared working week for those respondents who stated that they had carried out undeclared work, not for all 18–74-year-olds. The overall impact on the German economy must therefore be assessed by bringing these different figures together. This will be done in Chap. 7. It is, however, interesting to have a closer look at the socio-demographic structure of time spent on undeclared activities. This is done in Table 6.5.

Table 6.5 Average number of undeclared working hours, 18–74-years-olds who have carried out undeclared work, by gender, age and occupation, Germany, 2001 and 2004–2007

	Carried out undeclared work				
	2001	2004	2005	2006	2007
	%				
Men	8:27	7:52	8:14	6:19	6:33
Women	7:51	6:46	4:28	6:34	5:23
18–29-year-olds	7:39	7:30	6:59	(4:15)	6:14
30–39-year-olds	7:44	(12:49)	9:14	(6:54)	(8:57)
40–49-year-olds	9:01	5:33	5:45	(10:45)	(4:15)
50–59-year-olds	10:46	(7:02)	5:41	(5:18)	(7:39)
60–74-year-olds	7:18	(5:56)	3:59	(4:40)	(3:37)
Self-employed/assisting spouse	(13:13)	(27:06)	(2:48)	(16:01)	(7:53)
Salaried employees	4:03	(2:03)	5:54	(2:46)	(5:22)
Skilled workers	7:32	6:26	(6:50)	(5:55)	(3:55)
Unskilled workers	8:34	(11:16)	(6:38)	(3:57)	(5:26)
Unemployed	10:42	(5:54)	10:40	(5:55)	(12:26)
Pensioners	8:55	8:56	(3:47)	(3:43)	(2:49)
Students	8:41	(13:59)	(4:16)	(2:47)	(7:21)
Other	7:38	(7:51)	(10:05)	(16:13)	(7:02)
Total	8:14	7:30	6:40	6:25	6:16
Number of persons	5,686	2,143	2,144	2,176	1,096

Source: The Rockwool Foundation Research Unit's Shadow Economy Surveys

Note: Figures in brackets are based on less than 20 observations: i.e. less than 20 respondents answered one of the two questions about time spent on undeclared work (see the text). The sample has been drawn at the household level, and a weight has been applied to make the sample representative as to gender and age distribution and other characteristics of the total population

Generally, women who carry out undeclared work spend less time on these activities than men and this difference became more pronounced from the first survey in 2001 to the next surveys in 2004 and 2005. But in 2006 the difference between men and women apparently had disappeared: on average, women who carried out undeclared work spent just over 6½ per week and men spent just over 6¼ h. This is, however, due solely to the data collected in October of that year: according to the interviews carried out in September 2006, men spent 8¼ h and women spent 6 h. On the other hand, in two of the five waves of interviews in 2001, women also spent more time than men on average. In 2007, the average was about 6½ h for men and 1 h and 10 min less for women. Overall, this development represents a decrease from 2001 to 2007 for men – from 8 h and 27 min to 6 h and 33 min – as well as for women – from 7 h and 51 min to 5 h and 23 min. And as women reduced the time they spent on such activities more than men did over the period of the surveys, the relative difference between men and women in this regard, which from the outset in 2001 was relatively small, has become larger.

There are also marked structural differences in the age and occupational structure of the average number of undeclared working hours per week. Except for the 30–39-year-olds, which according to Table 6.2 (together with the 20–29-year-olds)

is the age group with the highest participation rate in 2007 and also (together with the 40–49 year-olds) the age group with the most stable participation rate, all age groups reduced their average number of undeclared weekly working hours during the period. The 40–49-year-olds who exhibited an unchanged rate of participation in undeclared work during the period had more than halved their time spent in 2007 compared with 2001 – from about 9 h to 4¼ h – but it seems that most of the change took place already from 2001 to 2005. An isolated increase in the undeclared working week to 10 h in the survey in 2006 confuses the picture for this group and the same does an exceptionally large number of hours in 2004 for the 30–39-year-olds.

The 18–29-year-olds reduced their average number of undeclared hours worked without declaration by about 1½ h from 2001 to 6¼ h in 2007. The 50–59-year-olds have experienced a U-shaped development from a very high level of 10 h in 2001 to 5¼ h in 2006 and then an increase to 7 h and 39 min in 2007, whereas the 60–74-year-olds have experienced a steadier decline from more than 7¼ h to just over 3½ h. In 2007, the 30–39-year-olds thus is the age group with the highest participation rate and the longest working week of all in the undeclared sector.

It should be noted that some of the reported averages, especially at the end of the period, are based on relatively few observations: if less than 20 persons answered one of the two questions about time spent on undeclared activities, then their average is put in brackets irrespective of the total number of persons in the group concerned who had carried out undeclared work. This is especially the case with respect to occupation and we therefore refrain from detailed remarks and interpretations on the self-employed and assisting spouses and students because these figures are based on few observations. The most notable example of this is the heavy increase for the self-employed from about 13½ h in 2001 to more than 27 h in 2004 which is based on only two people.

If the interviews in 2004 and 2005 are pooled in order to compare results based on more even sample sizes and identical field periods, our calculations show that the average undeclared working week was reduced for skilled workers by about 1 h between 2001 and 2004–2005 to 6 h, while pensioners reduced their hours worked in the undeclared part of the economy by more than 3 h to 5 h per week. Overall, the decline seems to have continued in 2006–2007 for both groups. The unemployed also experienced a decrease, when the average is calculated this way by pooling surveys, but their time spent varies more up and down from survey to survey than the undeclared working weeks of skilled workers and pensioners. The average undeclared working week remained constant for salaried employees at a little more than 4 h and for unskilled workers at 8½ h from 2001 to 2004–2005, if we, for the sake of the experiment, continue to regard the interviews in 2004 and 2005 as one survey. Calculated the same way by pooling 2006 and 2007, the level among salaried employees was stable during the whole period, whereas unskilled workers seem to have reduced the time they spent on undeclared activities at the end of the period. The actual figures for each year can be seen in Table 6.5.

6.4 Wages in Undeclared Work

A final ingredient required to calculate the economic importance of undeclared activities is still lacking. With information on the number of people participating in undeclared work and on the time these people spend per week on such activities, we have figures about the quantity of undeclared work. However, in a national accounts context, for example, economic importance is determined by the quantity and the actual price paid for the work or service. It is therefore necessary to obtain information on the monetary evaluation of undeclared work. It must be noted again that undeclared activities according to our definition comprise work for payments in cash as well as in the form of quid pro quos (return services, in kind), so that we had to pose questions on the average hourly wage for undeclared work for both types of undeclared activities. The questions in German read as follows:

> Wenn Sie an die Tätigkeiten denken, für die Sie in den vergangenen 12 Monaten mit Geld bezahlt wurden, das Sie nicht versteuert haben: Was schätzen Sie, ungefähr wie viel Euro haben Sie da im Durchschnitt pro Stunde erhalten?
>
> Wenn Sie für die Arbeiten auf Gegenleistung, die Sie in den letzten 12 Monaten gemacht haben, anstelle einer Gegenleistung mit Geld bezahlt worden wären: Was schätzen Sie, ungefähr wie viel Euro hätten Sie da im Durchschnitt pro Stunde erhalten?

The answers to these questions are summarized in Tables 6.6, 6.7, 6.8, 6.9 and 6.10.

Table 6.6 provides the overall information on the average hourly wages paid for undeclared work in Euro (in current prices). Amazingly, the hourly compensation remained virtually unchanged from 2001 to 2004, only increasing by ten cents from €10.30 to €10.40, but then increased to 12–13 Euros in 2005–2007. 2006 does not stand out in comparison with other years in terms of wages, but once again the

Table 6.6 Average hourly wages for undeclared work, 18–74-year-olds who have carried out undeclared work within the last year, Euro, Germany, 2001 and 2004–2007

	Euro (current prices)[a]	Number of persons who answered the questions about undeclared wages
2001	10.3	346
2004	10.4	130
2005	13.3	143
2006	11.8	94
2007	12.8	77

Source: The Rockwool Foundation Research Unit's Shadow Economy Surveys

Note: The sample has been drawn at the household level, and a weight has been applied to make the sample representative as to gender and age distribution and other characteristics of the total population. The number of persons shown in the table is the actual number before a weight was applied

[a]The average undeclared hourly wage rate in the national currency of DEM 20 in 2001 has been converted to Euro by using the average synthetic exchange rate in 2001

Table 6.7 Average hourly wages for undeclared work, 18–74-year-olds who have carried out undeclared work within the last year, by gender, age and occupation, Euro, Germany, 2001 and 2004–2007

	2001	2004	2005	2006	2007
	Euro (current prices)[a]				
Men	11.3	11.0	15.1	12.1	12.2
Women	8.4	8.7	10.0	11.1	15.6
18–29-year-olds	9.0	9.1	14.2	10.1	12.4
30–39-year-olds	11.3	11.9	13.7	12.8	(12.7)
40–49-year-olds	12.7	10.1	11.6	(14.3)	(16.7)
50–59-year-olds	9.7	(10.9)	13.8	(11.4)	(13.1)
60–74-year-olds	8.5	8.7	11.6	(10.9)	(8.4)
Self-employed/assisting spouse	15.1	(23.1)	(19.3)	(9.8)	(16.3)
Salaried employees	14.6	(11.5)	19.6	(12.5)	(16.4)
Skilled workers	11.1	12.0	(12.0)	12.4	(12.9)
Unskilled workers	8.6	(9.2)	(9.5)	(13.0)	(6.7)
Unemployed	8.2	6.8	9.9	(11.4)	(10.1)
Pensioners	8.1	8.3	9.9	(8.6)	(8.6)
Students	8.4	(11.3)	(10.2)	(11.7)	(15.1)
Other	8.4	(7.4)	(13.6)	(11.4)	(17.7)
Total	10.3	10.4	13.3	11.8	13.0
Number of persons who answered the questions about undeclared wages	346	130	143	94	77

Source: The Rockwool Foundation Research Unit's Shadow Economy Surveys
Note: Figures in brackets are based on less than 20 observations: i.e. less than 20 respondents answered the question about the monetary evaluation of the undeclared activities they had carried out (see the text). The sample has been drawn at the household level, and a weight has been applied to make the sample representative as to gender and age distribution and other characteristics of the total population
[a]The average hourly wage rate for undeclared work in the national currency of DEM 20 in 2001 has been converted to Euro by using the average synthetic exchange rate in 2001

Table 6.8 Average hourly wages for undeclared work, 18–74-year-olds who have carried out undeclared work within the last year, by form of payment, Euro, Germany, 2001 and 2004–2007

	2001	2004	2005	2006	2007
	Euro (current prices)[a]				
Cash	9.5	10.2	9.0	(9.2)	(11.7)
Quid pro quo	11.0	10.4	16.9	13.4	14.1
Both cash and quid pro quo	10.4	10.5	10.5	10.5	12.2
Total	10.3	10.4	13.3	11.8	13.0
Number of persons who answered the questions about undeclared wages	346	130	143	94	77

Source: The Rockwool Foundation Research Unit's Shadow Economy Surveys
Note: Figures in brackets are based on less than 20 observations: i.e. less than 20 respondents answered the question about the monetary evaluation of the undeclared activities they had carried out (see the text). The sample has been drawn at the household level, and a weight has been applied to make the sample representative as to gender and age distribution and other characteristics of the total population
[a]The average hourly wage rate for undeclared work in the national currency of DEM 20 in 2001 has been converted to Euro by using the average synthetic exchange rate in 2001

Table 6.9 Average hourly wages for undeclared work, 18–74-year-olds who have carried out undeclared work within the last year, by sector, Euro, Germany, 2001 and 2004–2007

	2001	2004	2005	2006	2007
	Euro (current prices)[a]				
Agriculture, fishing, quarrying	7.9	(9.5)	(12.3)	(13.5)	(11.7)
Manufacturing	(12.7)	(7.0)	(2.8)	(10.0)	(15.6)
Construction	11.5	11.1	11.7	12.2	(12.2)
Sales and repairs	(10.6)	(14.3)	(19.0)	(12.6)	(16.5)
Hotels and restaurants	(7.7)	(7.1)	(11.1)	(6.3)	(9.7)
Transport, telecommunications	(7.6)	(9.3)	(11.5)	(5.3)	(11.3)
Financial intermediation and business activities	10.2	(9.4)	20.4	(10.1)	(8.5)
Public and personal services	10.6	(8.6)	9.6	(13.6)	(21.2)
Not stated	10.6	(3.8)	(12.2)	(5.0)	(13.0)
Total	10.3	10.4	13.3	11.8	13.0
Number of persons who answered the questions about undeclared wages	346	130	143	94	74

Source: The Rockwool Foundation Research Unit's Shadow Economy Surveys
Note: Figures in brackets are based on less than 20 observations: i.e. less than 20 respondents answered the question about the monetary evaluation of the undeclared activities they had carried out (see the text). The sample has been drawn at the household level, and a weight has been applied to make the sample representative as to gender and age distribution and other characteristics of the total population. The classification of sectors follows the nine-sector grouping in NACE, rev. 1, except that "hotels and restaurants" are split off on their own. Moreover, the "electricity and gas supply" sector is omitted, since there are no undeclared activities in this sector
[a]The average hourly wage rate for undeclared work in the national currency of DEM 20 in 2001 has been converted to Euro by using the average synthetic exchange rate in 2001

responses in the interviews carried out in October revealed a significantly lower average than was the case for the interviews carried out in September.

The consistency of these figures is underlined by the structural information provided in Table 6.7. For men and for women, average undeclared hourly wages remained almost unchanged between 2001 and 2004 at around 11 Euros and 8½ Euros respectively, whereas men in particular benefited from the increase from 2004 to 2005. In all 3 years, then, women earned less in the undeclared sector of the economy than men, a finding that reflects the situation in the official economy, and the difference actually increased in 2005: on average, men earned one third more than women in 2001, but 50% more in 2005.

However, in the most recent surveys in 2006 and 2007 the differential appears to have (practically) disappeared. The single wave of interviews in 2007 even indicated that women then earned more than men, but too much emphasis on that result may lead to premature conclusions: a small number of respondents reporting relatively, but not unrealistically high wages may pull the average up to a comparatively high level, and such an effect may be the result of chance, unless the number of interviews is very large. But if we, to be on the safe side, assume that the average remuneration for women was the same in 2007 as in 2006 – i.e. about 11 Euros – then women still have experienced a steady increase – from €8.4 to €11.1 – whereas men

Table 6.10 Proportion of the population in the 18–74 age group who has carried out undeclared work within the last year and average monthly income from undeclared work by the household's net income in the formal economy, Germany, 2001 and 2004–2007

Household's net income in the formal economy per month in Euro	Proportion who has carried out undeclared work					Average undeclared income per month among those who have carried out undeclared work				
	2001	2004	2005	2006	2007	2001	2004	2005	2006	2007
	%					Euro (current prices)[a]				
0–499	(11.9)	(14.9)	(15.5)	(8.6)	(10.3)	(381)	(129)	(182)	(163)	(1,011)
500–999	11.3	13.7	14.0	8.4	14.1	365	(336)	(213)	(100)	(215)
1,000–1,499	11.0	9.1	10.5	5.6	12.0	287	(677)	(352)	(193)	(65)
1,500–1,999	8.9	5.5	9.9	5.9	10.3	246	(585)	(235)	(147)	(427)
2,000+	8.9	7.7	9.7	5.4	6.6	406	224	296	370	(223)
Total	9.7	8.5	10.6	6.0	9.6	343	374	277	234	284
	Sample size					Answered the questions about undeclared wages				
Number of persons	5,686	2,141	2,136	2,172	1,096	243	83	100	62	56

Source: The Rockwool Foundation Research Unit's Shadow Economy Surveys

Note: Figures in brackets are based on less than 20 observations: i.e. less than 20 respondents answered the question about the monetary evaluation of the undeclared activities they had carried out (see the text). Average monthly income from undeclared activities has been calculated on the basis of the observed hourly wages for undeclared work and the number of hours of undeclared work per week times 52/12. The proportions of the population have been calculated for those with an observed income from the formal part of the economy and may therefore differ from the other tables. *As this table is based on households rather than persons, no weight has been applied*

[a]The average hourly wage rate for undeclared work in the national currency of DEM 20 in 2001 has been converted to Euro by using the average synthetic exchange rate in 2001

have only experienced a rather small increase – from €11.3 to €12.2 – and the gender differential in terms of wage level has become almost negligible.

The overall remuneration thus remained very stable from 2001 to 2004; the same is true of the wages received by different age groups. There is only one notable exception: the average undeclared hourly wages for the 40–49-year-olds declined from €12.70 to €10.10. A comparison of the compensation patterns across age groups does not show important differences in either of the two years, again with the exception of the 40–49-year-olds, who earned about 50% more than the 60–74-year-olds in 2001. In 2004, the 30–39-year-olds earned the highest average undeclared hourly wages with €11.90, which is more than 3 Euros more than the compensation for the 60–74-year-olds, who remained at the lower end of the wage scale.

This picture changed somewhat from 2004 to 2005, mainly resulting in a reduction of the wage dispersion on the undeclared labor market via a general wage increase which benefited all groups, but which favored those most who had the lowest initial wages, i.e. the 18–29-year-olds and the 50–74-year-olds. The results of the 2007 survey suggest that by then the 60–74-year-olds had lost what they had gained in 2005, while the 40–49-year-olds had experienced a further increase, and the rest of the groups had lost some, but not all they had gained in 2005. All age groups had thus lost relative to the 40–49-year-olds. It must be remembered, of course, that the survey in 2007 consisted of only one wave of interviews and that calculations based on a larger sample may show a reduction in these apparent changes.

The issue of sample sizes is more significant for an examination of the differences across occupational groups and across these groups over time. Again we refrain from detailed remarks and interpretations on the self-employed and students due to relatively few cell entries. When the various surveys are compared, the picture with regard to groups below and above the average is relatively unchanged. Salaried employees and skilled workers raise the average (though only slightly in the case of the latter), while unskilled workers, pensioners and the unemployed lower it. Skilled workers had a very stable level of wages, increasing slowly but steadily from €11.1 in 2001 to €12.9 in 2007, and also the wages of the unemployed and pensioners remained relatively stable and without the large fluctuations, which the other occupational groups exhibit from time to time.

In Table 6.8 we distinguish the average undeclared hourly wages according to the two different kinds of undeclared activities, those paid for in cash and those paid for in kind (or a quid pro quo or return service). The third group comprises those people who worked for payments both in cash and in kind. While there were only negligible differences between the groups in 2001 and virtually no differences in 2004, there were notable differences in 2005, where the average hourly compensation for activities paid for with a quid pro quo suddenly increased by more than 50%, from €10.4 to €16.9. The results of the surveys in 2006 and 2007 confirm this increase, though not its size. Compared with those paid for in kind, those paid in cash may be said to have received a stable level of pay, as their rates lie within the interval €9.0 to €10.2, increasing slightly to €11.7 in 2007. However, those who received a combination of cash and quid pro quo had an even more stable average level of pay of 10½ Euro per hour in each year surveyed, increasing slightly to €12.2 in 2007. The result of this is that the three groups approach each other again after 2005 but at a somewhat higher level.

The averages for hourly undeclared wages by sector, as reported in Table 6.9, are also heavily affected by the small number of entries in the different cells. The marked differences for some sectors over time and across groups may thus also be attributable to the small (sub) sample factor.

It is noteworthy that the most important sector with respect to undeclared activities – the construction sector – is characterized by a very stable rate of pay of between €11.1 and €12.2, which very much resembles that of skilled workers (see Table 6.7). Though much of the work in the construction sector is not carried out by skilled workers or people who normally work in the construction sector, these almost identical levels and paths may be seen as a validation of the answers to the questions about undeclared wages.

The agricultural sector (including gardening) also exhibits a relatively even progression from an average payment of €7.9 in 2001 to €11.7 in 2007. If we ignore the results of the survey in 2006, hotels and restaurants and transport/telecommunications can be seen to have followed similar paths, from an average hourly wage between 7 and 8 Euros in 2001 to about 10 and 11 Euros in 2007. The only sector with a constant average hourly payment above the average is sales and repairs.

6.5 Undeclared Activities by Income Class

A final highlight of our differentiated descriptive analysis is provided in Table 6.10. In the left part of the table there is information on the proportion of the population who has carried out undeclared work, and in the right part of the table there is information on the average monthly income from undeclared work, both grouped according to the different *household* net income classes. *Note that unlike the rest of the tables, this table is at the household level.* The figures on the share of people engaged in undeclared activities indicate the tendency towards a negative influence of income on the probability of participating in such activities which was also noticed in the regression analysis in Sect. 6.2.

The income earned from undeclared work in addition to that in the official economy does not follow such a trend at all. There appears to be a U-shaped bivariate relationship between income and additional monthly earnings in 2001, with a local minimum in the middle income group and a global maximum in the highest income group. In 2004 and 2005, most notably in 2004, there are high additional incomes in the middle income classes, i.e. a reversed U-shaped bivariate relationship between income and additional monthly earnings; in 2005 it is only approximately so. If 2004 and 2005 are regarded as one survey, they generate a perfect reversed U-shaped relationship. In 2006, the structure is very similar to that in 2005 as the differences in additional income earned from undeclared work in the various groups are relatively small, there is a local maximum in the middle income group, but the global maximum is in the highest income group. Finally, in 2007, the relationship is approximately U-shaped with the lowest income supplement found in the middle income class, but there is neither a global nor a local maximum in the highest income class. Across time, there appear to be strong increases and decreases. At first glance, it looks as though the highest and the lowest income classes have lost some of the amount of additional income from undeclared work, while the middle income classes seem to have gained.

6.6 Summarizing the Main Findings

The average rate of participation in undeclared work varies around an average which would be one in ten had it not been for the results of two waves of interviews carried out in 2006 which pull the average down. The rate among men is about 40–50% higher than the average for all 18–74-year-olds, and thus much higher than among women, and women apparently have reduced their participation at the end of the period.

At the beginning of the period, the highest participation rates are found in the youngest age groups, but the 18–29-year-olds appear to have reduced their participation to a level close to that of the 30–39-year-olds who are characterized by a remarkably stable participation rate of about 12–13%. A remarkable stability is also characteristic of the 40–49-year-olds at a somewhat lower level of about

9–11% as participation is decreasing by age. Generally, the occupational groups with the highest representation on the undeclared labor market have been skilled workers, the unemployed and students.

The average time spent per week on undeclared work was gradually reduced from 8¼ h per week in 2001 to 6¼ h in 2007. Men who carry out undeclared work spend more time on such activities than women, and the relative difference has become larger, as men reduced their undeclared working week from 8½ to 6½ h, while women reduced their undeclared working week from just under 8 h to just under 5½ h. Except for the 30–39-year-olds who increased average time spent to almost 9 h per week, all other age groups reduced their average number of undeclared working hours per week during the period. In 2007, the 30–39-year-olds thus is the age group with the highest participation rate, together with the 20–29-year-olds, and the longest working week in the undeclared sector of the economy. It should be noted, however, that the survey in 2007 is based on only one wave consisting of about 1,100 interviews.

Skilled workers and pensioners experienced a constant and significant reduction of their undeclared working hours per week from 2001 to positions below the average for all 18–74-year-olds in 2007, salaried employees remained constant and below the average for all, while unskilled workers moved from a position above the average in the surveys in 2001 and 2004 to a position below the average at the end of he period. The average working week for the relatively large proportion of the unemployed participating in undeclared activities is above the average for all 18–74-year-olds but also varies more up and down than in the other groups just mentioned.

The hourly compensation for undeclared work remained virtually unchanged from 2001 to 2004 at just under 10½ Euro, but then increased to 12–13 Euros in 2005–2007. At the beginning of the period, men had an hourly wage of about 11 Euros, while women earned about 8½ Euro an hour. Whereas men benefited most from a wage increase from 2004 to 2005, the gender differential appears to have become almost negligible in 2006 and even reversed in 2007, but again it is necessary to make reservations for the somewhat ambiguous results of the surveys in 2006 and the relatively small number of interviews in 2007.

The lowest hourly wages are earned by the youngest and the oldest age groups in the majority of the surveys, but this picture changed somewhat from 2004 to 2005, mainly resulting in a reduction of the undeclared wage dispersion via a general wage increase which benefited all groups, but which favored those most who had the lowest initial wages, but this trend seems to have been reversed in the latest surveys where all groups, and the 60–74-year-olds in particular, lost relative to the 40–49-year-olds. Salaried employees and skilled workers raise the wage level, while unskilled workers, pensioners and the unemployed lower it. Skilled workers had a very stable level of wages, increasing slowly but steadily from €11.1 in 2001 to €12.9 in 2007, and also the wages of the unemployed and pensioners remained relatively stable and without the large fluctuations, which the other occupational groups exhibit from time to time. Again we refrain from detailed remarks and interpretations on the self-employed and students due to the relatively few respondents in these groups who reported wages for undeclared work.

With regard to form of payment, those paid in cash – €9.0 to €10.2, increasing slightly to €11.7 in 2007 – and those who received a combination of cash and quid pro quo (return services, payment in kind) – 10½ Euro per hour in each year surveyed, increasing slightly to €12.2 in 2007 – have received a stable level of pay compared with those paid only in kind or return services. While there were only negligible differences between the groups in 2001 and virtually no differences in 2004, there were notable differences in 2005, when the average hourly compensation for activities paid for with a quid pro quo suddenly increased by more than 50%, from €10.4 to €16.9. The results of the surveys in 2006 and 2007 confirm this increase, though not its size.

It is noteworthy that the most important sector with respect to undeclared work – the construction sector – is characterized by a very stable rate of pay of between €11.1 and €12.2, and the agricultural sector (including gardening) also exhibits a relatively even progression from an average payment of €7.9 in 2001 to €11.7 in 2007. Sales and repairs is the only sector with a constant average hourly payment above the average for all.

Finally, data indicate a tendency towards a decrease in the probability of participating in undeclared work with rising household income in the official economy. The income earned from undeclared work in addition to that in the official economy does not appear to follow such a trend.

A rather preliminary econometric analysis with the purpose of establishing correlations of socio-economic explanatory variables and the year of the survey with participation (1) as opposed to not participating (0) in undeclared work led to the following observations: the probability of having carried out undeclared work is higher for men younger than the reference group chosen, which is the 40–49-year-olds, and lower for those who are older, single women are more likely to carry out undeclared work than married women and being a skilled worker irrespective of gender, an unskilled woman or a female student also is correlated with undeclared work. The most significant effect as far as education is concerned is that men who have completed Fachschule (secondary school) have a significantly higher probability of having carried out undeclared work than the reference group with a beruflich-betriebliche education (dual education) and low income also increases the probability. In case of unemployment, the length of the period without a job increases the probability, but only for men. Finally, women's participation is significantly lower at the end of the period than at the beginning while it cannot be rejected that the participation rate for men has been constant throughout the period.

It should be noted that in the econometric analysis in this chapter we have pooled all our data sets into one. There are differences in the estimation results from year to year, e.g., as far as occupation is concerned, if the regressions are performed for each year separately instead. In later chapters we will try other specifications of the model and add qualitative variables in order to capture the effect of deterrence, tax policy and social norms.

Chapter 7
The Extent of Undeclared Work in Germany 2001–2007

7.1 Undeclared Work as a Share of the Official Economy

In Chap. 6 we calculated the incidence of undeclared work, i.e. how many people are involved, how much time they spend on such activities each week, and how much they are paid or receive in return. With this information we have a means of estimating the total extent of undeclared work. One way is to calculate the total number of hours spent on such activities in 1 year as a proportion of the total number of declared hours worked in the formal economy. This corresponds to measuring the undeclared sector relative to official GDP on the assumption that productivity is the same in the informal sector as in the formal economy within the various trades and industries or sectors, and also that overall average productivity or value added across trades and industries is the same.

In favor of this assumption would be a higher after-tax payment, the element of choice, and, probably, a greater motivation in the informal sector than in the formal economy. Also, the fact that undeclared work is often carried out in the evening and at weekends may be an incentive to be efficient in order to ensure some leisure time. If undeclared work is carried out in connection with an ongoing project which for the most part lies in the formal economy, then most of the costs will also be declared, so the marginal costs of hiring someone to do a smaller part of the job without declaration probably will be below the average costs for the whole project.

Against the assumption that the value added per hour worked is the same, it may be argued that the amount and standard of capital equipment at the disposal for undeclared workers is less than that for workers in the formal economy, though to some extent the same workshops, tools, and vans, etc., are used in both sectors. The fact that a large proportion of this kind of work is carried out by persons who are not trained for it also reduces productivity.

In Table 7.1 working hours spent on undeclared work and on the formal labor market respectively are used to estimate the size of the undeclared sector as a percentage relative to GDP. Both official and unofficial working hours are reported by the respondents in the interviews. The total number of hours worked in the

L.P. Feld and C. Larsen, *Undeclared Work, Deterrence and Social Norms*,
DOI 10.1007/978-3-540-87401-0_7,

Table 7.1 Average number of undeclared working hours per week as a proportion of declared working hours, 18–66-year-olds, Germany, 2001 and 2004–2007

	Frequency of doing undeclared work	Average undeclared working hours per week, persons who have carried out undeclared work	Average undeclared working hours per week, total population	Average normal declared working hours per week, total population[a]	Undeclared working hours as a proportion of declared hours ("percent of GDP")
	1	2	$3 = (1\times2)\times100$	4	$5 = 3/4$
	Proportion %	Hours per week[b]	Hours per week[b]	Hours per week[b]	Proportion %
2001	11.7	8.31	0.97	23.6	4.11
2004	9.6	7.56	0.73	23.4	3.12
2005	12.2	6.80	0.83	23.4	3.55
2006	6.3	6.52	0.41	22.4	1.83
2007	10.7	6.26	0.67	21.1	3.18

Source: The Rockwool Foundation Research Unit's Shadow Economy Surveys
Note: The sample has been drawn at the household level, and a weight has been applied to make the sample representative as to gender and age distribution and other characteristics of the total population. As the comparison is with the formal labor market the age group in this table is 18–66 years
[a]Number of hours worked in main and secondary jobs in the formal economy according to statements by the respondents in the surveys
[b]Minutes expressed as percentages of an hour

official economy by those in employment is divided by the total number of 18–66-year-old respondents in the survey—employed as well as unemployed. As the comparison is with average working weeks on the formal labor market, the age group in Tables 7.1 and 7.5 is 18–66 years, whereas it is 18–74 years in the rest of the tables. The participation rates and time spent thus may differ from the figures in Chap. 6.

As shown in Chap. 6, the proportion of the population who had carried out undeclared work, as well as the average number of hours spent on such activities, decreased from 2001 to 2004. At the same time, normal declared average weekly working hours reported by the respondents in the surveys amounted to 23 h and 24 min in 2004 compared with 23 h and 36 min in 2001, which may be explained by the rise in unemployment in Germany in the same period. Overall, this resulted in a 24% decrease in the extent of undeclared work measured relative to GDP in Germany from 4.1% in 2001 to 3.1% in 2004.

In 2005, the rate of participation increased again, but even though it increased to the highest level measured in these surveys, undeclared work "only" reached 3.6% measured as a percentage of declared working hours ("percent of GDP"), because average undeclared weekly working hours continued to decrease. The average undeclared working week also decreased in 2006 and 2007 and, as explained in Chap. 6, two surveys carried out in 2006 resulted in an unusually low participation rate. Undeclared hours as a proportion of declared working hours therefore decreased to 1.83% in 2006—the lowest level measured in these surveys—in spite of a 1 h decrease in the working week on the formal labor market. Finally, in 2007, a participation rate of 10.7% among the 18–66-year-olds combined with an average undeclared working week of now just over 6¼ h resulted in an undeclared sector which amounted to 3.18% relative to GDP.

The calculations in Table 7.1 correspond to estimating what the activities could be worth if they were carried out in the formal economy at normal market prices. Alternatively, the size of the undeclared sector can be calculated by using the actual prices paid, which, by definition, are lower than the market prices (for similar services or goods delivered at the same time and at the same place via the formal economy). This is done in Table 7.2 and results in estimates which are about two thirds lower than those in Table 7.1. The estimate was reduced by 25% from 1.3% relative to GDP in 2001 to 1.0% in 2004. However, this was *more* than offset in 2005 when the proportion reached about 1.4%. The lowest level—0.6%—is found in 2006, but, as mentioned, an important question to investigate is how much of this decrease is actually due to changes in the level of participation in undeclared activities and how much is caused by other things. In 2007, undeclared working hours times actual prices paid for undeclared work corresponded to 1% of the official GDP.

It should be noted that national statistical bureaus include estimates of the shadow economy in the national accounts via various explicit and implicit allowances to achieve exhaustiveness and as true and fair a view of the economy as possible (OECD 2002). Adding official GDP and estimates of undeclared work would thus lead to an overestimation of the total economic activity and therefore we use expressions like undeclared work "relative to official GDP" or "in percent of GDP".

Table 7.2 Extent of undeclared work based on actual prices paid in the undeclared economy, 18–74-year-olds, Germany, 2001 and 2004–2007

	Number of undeclared working hours per year	Average hourly wage for undeclared work	Extent of undeclared work at actual prices paid	Extent of undeclared work at actual prices paid as a proportion of GDP[a]
	Million hours[b]	Euro[c]	Million Euros[c]	%
2001	2,707.2	10.3	27,884	1.32
2004	2,096.6	10.4	21,805	0.99
2005	2,352.6	13.3	31,290	1.39
2006	1,183.9	11.8	13,970	0.60
2007	1,935.7	12.8	24,777	1.02

Source: The Rockwool Foundation Research Unit's Shadow Economy Surveys

[a]GDP (million Euros) from Eurostat http://epp.eurostat.ec.europa.eu (Data—Economy and finance—National accounts (including GDP)): 2001: 2.113.160, 2004: 2.210.900, 2005: 2.243.200, 2006: 2.321.500, 2007: 2.422.900

[b]Frequency of doing undeclared work/100 × average number of undeclared working hours per week by persons who have carried out undeclared work × 52 × total population aged 18–74 on 1 January. Population, 18–74 years, from Eurostat http://epp.eurostat.ec.europa.eu (Data—Population and social conditions—Population): 2001: 60.825.462, 2004: 61.090.674, 2005: 61.107.853, 2006: 61.144.646, 2007: 61.204.638

[c]The monthly incomes in DEM in 2001 have been converted to Euro by using the synthetic average exchange rate for 2001

As emphasized previously, both measures of undeclared activities should be considered minimum estimates, since some people may not give an honest answer as to whether they carry out such activities or not, and some may not admit the true extent of their engagement even though they are guaranteed anonymity. A decrease in the total size of the undeclared sector from 2001 to 2004 might be expected in the light of the considerable legislative activity and campaigns against undeclared work (and other kinds of tax evasion) since 2001, but, as was also emphasized previously, the decrease may reflect both an actual change in respondents' behavior in the shadow economy and a change in their readiness to answer questions about it, and it is not possible to separate these two effects. The subsequent resurgence in 2005, the dramatic decrease in 2006 and the immediate increase in 2007 also suggest such a mixture of occasional and apparently partly transitory effects of the announcement of steps to enhance tax compliance, e.g. by raising the level of deterrence. However, it is not possible to point out particular events which can explain why this minimum level is reached exactly in 2006. Experience from Danish surveys carried out after the introduction in 2004 of a "Fairplay campaign" against undeclared work is the same: campaigns may have an effect on the survey results but the effects are to some extent temporary and depend on the intensity and media coverage of the campaign.

A third way to illustrate the extent of undeclared work is to "convert" the number of hours worked without declaration per year in Table 7.2 to full-time jobs. Of course, this is not the same as saying that all undeclared activities would automatically be carried out on the formal market instead, if we supposed for the sake of argument that from one day to the next nobody was willing to carry out undeclared work. In surveys by the Rockwool Foundation Research Unit in Denmark in 1999 (Pedersen 2003) and 2010 (Hvidtfeldt et al. 2010), questions were asked about the *demand* for undeclared purchase or acquisition of goods or services. Nearly two thirds of the respondents purchasing at that market stated that they would have done the work themselves instead, or that the transaction would not have taken place, if they had not been able to buy without declaration. In the Eurobarometer (2007) which we referred to in Chap. 3, 54% of the Danish respondents who had acquired goods or services which they had "a good reason to assume ... embodied undeclared work" answered that they would alternatively have bought the good or service from the regular market, while it was 34% of the German respondents (p. 13 and QB8-QB9).

Had all undeclared hours worked in 2001 been transferred to the formal economy, it would have corresponded to 1.63 million full-time jobs. This is based on an average normal number of working hours per year in a full-time job in Germany in 2001 as being 1,661, the figure given by the Institut für Arbeitsmarkt- und Berufsforschung (IAB 2008). If, more realistically, perhaps one third could be converted to work in the formal economy, it would still amount to more than 500,000 jobs. In 2004, undeclared work corresponded to 1.25 million full-time jobs (one third of which amounts to about 420,000 jobs). This is based on an average normal number of working hours per year in a full-time job at 1,678.4. In 2005, 2006, and 2007, similar calculations result in 1.40 million (465,000), 0.71 million (235,000), and 1.15 million (385,000) jobs respectively (see Table 7.3).

Table 7.3 Total number of undeclared hours worked per year converted to full-time jobs, 18–74-year olds, Germany, 2001 and 2004–2007

	Number of undeclared hours worked per year Million hours[a]	Number of full-time jobs if all undeclared hours were transferred to the formal economy Million full-time jobs[b]	Number of full-time jobs if one third of all undeclared hours were transferred to the formal economy
2001	2,707.2	1.63	543,000
2004	2,096.6	1.25	417,000
2005	2,352.6	1.40	467,000
2006	1,183.9	0.71	237,000
2007	1,935.7	1.15	383,000

Source: The Rockwool Foundation Research Unit's Shadow Economy Surveys

[a]Frequency of doing undeclared work/100 × average number of undeclared working hours per week by persons who have carried out undeclared work × 52 × total population aged 18–74 on 1 January. Population, 18–74 years, from Eurostat's homepage http://epp.eurostat.ec.europa.eu (Data—Population and social conditions—Population): 2001: 60.825.462, 2004: 61.090.674, 2005: 61.107.853, 2006: 61.144.646, 2007: 61.204.638.

[b]Average normal number of working hours per year in a full-time job from IAB (2008): 2001: 1,660.7, 2004: 1,678.4, 2005: 1,674.6, 2006: 1,678.5, 2007: 1,681.5

In a national accounts context, the extent of the undeclared sector of the economy measured at the actual prices and wages paid—i.e. the estimates shown in Table 7.2—would be relevant, since, by convention, the national accounts value any activity at the actual prices paid, and, as mentioned above, allowance is actually made for such activities as well as for "ordinary tax evasion"—i.e. non-declaration of sales and services at full market price where only the seller benefits—in the national accounts. A number of Norwegian studies during the 1980s and in 2001 (Isachsen and Strøm 1985; Goldstein 1990; Ognedal et al. 2002) estimate that ordinary tax evasion in Norway amounts to about one third of the size of undeclared activities approximately as defined here. According to Larsen (2002) and Viby Mogensen (2003) the extent of ordinary tax evasion may be estimated at 44% of the extent of undeclared work.

If the same applied to Germany, calculated at market prices, this would lead to an estimate of "undeclared personal income" in 2001 of 1.44 times 4.1% of GDP, i.e. 5.9%, compared to 1.44 times 3.1%, i.e. 4.5% of GDP, in 2004. In 2005, 2006, and 2007, similar calculations result in an amount of unreported income corresponding to 5.1, 2.6, and 4.6% of official GDP in Germany. It should be noted that this measure relates to unreported *personal* income. Tax evasion by companies, for example, is not included, though part of the "undeclared economy" may relate to activities arranged via the respondent's main job, or it may even be arranged by his or her employer—either in the sense that one of the conditions of employment in the company is that it is not reported to the authorities, or in the sense that the employer lets the person do some work for a third party and leaves it up to them to agree on the terms. The latter may happen if the company has too much to do to accept the piece of work in question on normal terms and conditions.

In spite of the fact that, so far, decreases have been followed by increases every second year, the estimates of the total number of undeclared hours, as well as the monetary evaluation of these activities, seem to indicate a slightly downward trend in the extent of undeclared work in Germany because decreases have not been fully offset the year after. The downward trend is due primarily to a continuously reduced average number of hours spent on undeclared work by people engaged in such activities, whereas the participation rate has varied more up and down. It may still be one in ten of the 18–74-year-olds who carry out undeclared work at least once during a 12 months period, but they are, on average, doing it for fewer hours. In addition to investigating which factors influence the decision whether or not to carry out undeclared work, another aspect of interest thus is which factors influence the number of hours worked undeclared once the decision to carry out such activities has been made. However, such an analysis is outside the scope of this study.

7.2 The Willingness to Carry Out Undeclared Work: The "Potential"

In order to get an idea of the potential for undeclared work, respondents who had *not* carried out any undeclared work within the last 12 months were asked if they would be willing to do so if the opportunity arose:

> Would you be willing—if you had the chance—to carry out undeclared work?

In a comparison of 2001 with 2004, the most notable finding that emerges from Table 7.4 is the increase in the proportion of the respondents who answered "no" from 61% to 68% and the proportional decrease for those that did not know or who refused to answer from 22% to 15%. The percentage who would be willing to carry out undeclared work if the opportunity arose was about 17% in both years. It is remarkable that the proportion increased to almost 20% in 2005—the year with the

Table 7.4 Willingness to carry out undeclared work if the opportunity arose among persons who have not carried out any undeclared work within the last 12 months, 18–74-year-olds, Germany, 2001 and 2004–2007, in percent

	Yes	No	Don't know/refusal	Total	No. of persons
2001	17.3	60.9	21.8	100	5,135
2004	17.1	68.0	14.9	100	1,961
2005	19.8	63.4	16.8	100	1,917
2006	15.5	71.9	12.6	100	2,045
2007	18.2	66.3	15.6	100	991

Source: The Rockwool Foundation Research Unit's Shadow Economy Surveys

Note: The sample has been drawn at the household level, and a weight has been applied to make the sample representative as to gender and age distribution and other characteristics of the total population. The number of persons shown in the table is the actual number before the weight was applied

Table 7.5 Carried out or would carry out undeclared work if the opportunity arose, 18–74-year-olds, Germany, 2001 and 2004–2007, in percent

	Carry out undeclared work	Do not carry out undeclared work, but would be willing to	Do not carry out undeclared work, and would not be willing to	Don't know/ refusal	Total	No. of persons
2001	10.4	15.1	54.2	20.3	100	5,686
2004	8.8	15.6	61.9	13.7	100	2,143
2005	11.1	17.5	56.3	15.0	100	2,144
2006	5.8	14.5	67.7	11.9	100	2,176
2007	9.7	16.3	59.9	14.1	100	1,096

Source: The Rockwool Foundation Research Unit's Shadow Economy Surveys
Note: The sample has been drawn at the household level, and a weight has been applied to make the sample representative as to gender and age distribution and other characteristics of the total population. The number of persons shown in the table is the actual number before the weight was applied

highest rate of participation—and that the lowest "potential" is found in 2006—the year with the lowest participation rate. In 2007, 18.2% of those who had not carried out undeclared work within the last 12 months said that they would be willing to do so if the opportunity arose.

All in all, as can be seen from Table 7.5, the proportion who either had carried out undeclared work or would be willing to do so if given the chance decreased from 25.5% in 2001 to 24.4% in 2004, while the proportion who neither had done nor would undertake undeclared work increased from 54.2% to 61.9%. In 2005, the proportion consisting of actual and potential participants increased to 28.6%; 56.3% answered "no" to both questions. In 2006 and 2007, actual and potential participants were 20.3 and 26.0 respectively; 67.7 and 59.9% answered "no" to both questions.

When we take this additional information from our surveys into consideration, we still reach the same overall assessment: the scale of undeclared work fell between 2001 and 2004. Again, this may (also) reflect an increased focus on the topic. On the other hand, the actual and potential participation rates, though not the total amount of undeclared work measured in hours, both reached their highest level in these surveys in 2005. The dramatic decrease in 2006 in the actual participation rate is not followed by an equally dramatic decrease in the proportion of respondents who would be willing to carry out undeclared work.

Whether a decrease in the rate of potential participation is to be expected or not, when actual participation decreases, depends on what has caused this decrease. If deterrence has, then the potential might still be there, or be even larger, but if it is tax morale or tax policy, then the potential probably would be smaller, too. In any case, the proportion who answered no both to the question about actual behavior and to the question about potential behavior reached its maximum in 2006, and the "don't know"-answers and refusals reached their minimum. That indicates a clearer and more dismissive attitude towards undeclared work but as this development was immediately reversed in 2007 the answer probably is not that straightforward.

7.3 Undeclared Work by Sector

Figures 7.1 and 7.2 indicate undeclared activities by sector. While the first figure shows the distribution of the total number of undeclared hours worked by sector in percent, the second shows undeclared hours worked as a proportion of registered working hours in the formal part of the economy in each sector.

From the data in Fig. 7.1, it is evident that the construction sector was the one with the largest amount of undeclared activities during the period 2001–2007. Its share of the total number of undeclared hours worked ranged from 27% to 54%. The true range certainly is narrower than that, and the peaks are to some extent due to underreporting in other sectors or other things which make the construction sector look relatively larger than it actually is. As we have seen above, the self-employed/assisting spouses group was practically absent in the informal sector in 2004, and Fig. 7.1 reveals that part of the explanation may be sought in agriculture, fishing, and quarrying (including gardening), collectively also known as the primary sector of the economy. On the other hand, undeclared hours in the primary sector as a percentage of all undeclared hours that year was also very low in 2007—the year

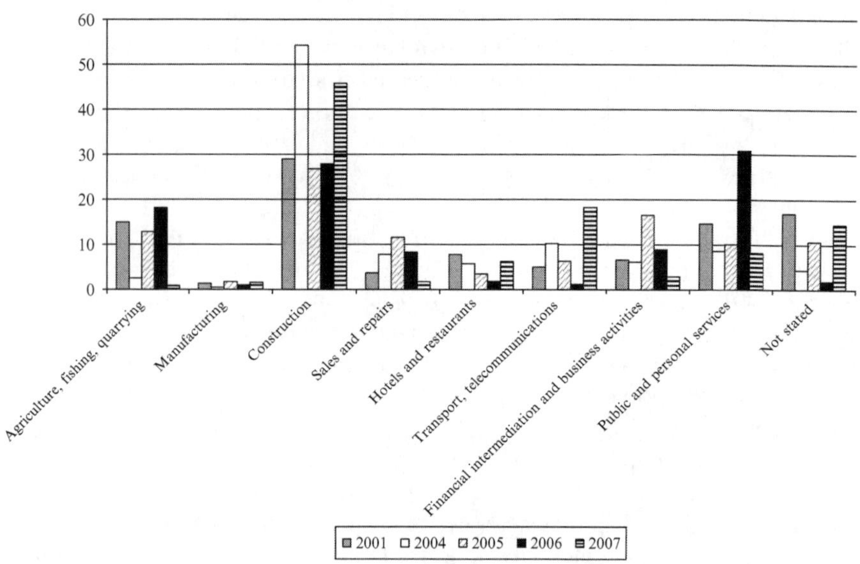

Fig. 7.1 The distribution of the total number of undeclared hours worked by sector, 18–74-year-olds, Germany, 2001 and 2004–2007, in percent. Notes: The sum of the columns each year equals 100. The sample has been drawn at the household level, and a weight has been applied to make the sample representative as to gender and age distribution and other characteristics of the total population. The classification by sector follows the nine-sector grouping in NACE, rev. 1, except that "hotels and restaurants" are split off on their own. Moreover, the electricity and gas supply sector is omitted, since there are no undeclared activities in this sector (Source: The Rockwool Foundation Research Unit's Shadow Economy Surveys)

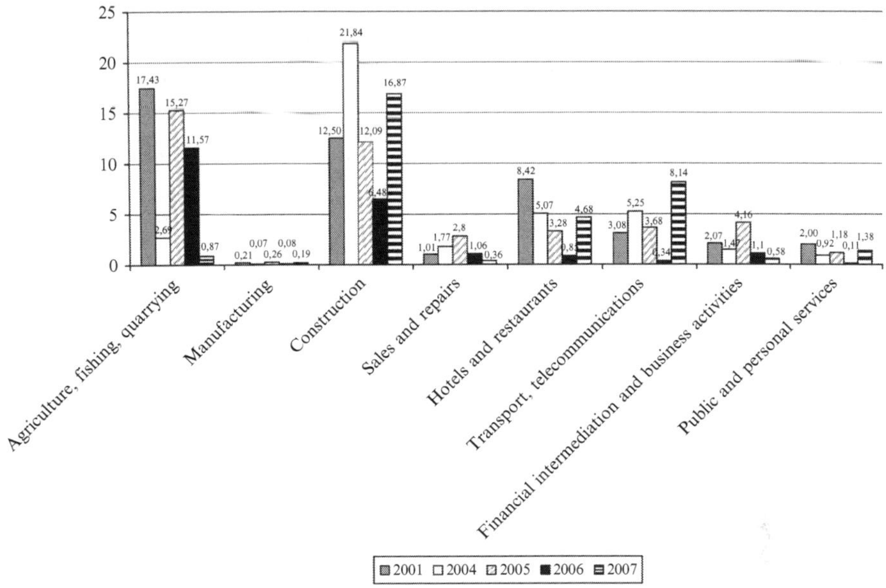

Fig. 7.2 Undeclared hours worked as a proportion of registered working hours in the formal part of the economy by sector, 18–74-year-olds, Germany, 2001 and 2004–2007, in percent. Notes: The sample has been drawn at the household level, and a weight has been applied to make the sample representative as to gender and age distribution and other characteristics of the total population. The classification by sector follows the nine-sector grouping in NACE, rev. 1, except that "hotels and restaurants" are split off. Moreover, the electricity and gas supply sector is omitted, since there are no undeclared activities in this sector. The figures for hours worked by sector in the formal economy are from Eurostat's homepage http://epp.eurostat.ec.europa.eu (Data—Population and social conditions—Labour market) and are for the 15–64-year-olds (Source: The Rockwool Foundation Research Unit's Shadow Economy Surveys)

with the *highest* participation rate among the self-employed/assisting spouses found in these surveys.

The distribution in Fig. 7.1 is based on information about participation rates *and* undeclared hours worked *and* types of activity (sector). Many of the columns therefore are based on answers from relatively few, or even very few, persons. Few persons who work many hours thus can result in a sudden increase or decrease in the proportion made up by a particular sector. Nevertheless, Fig. 7.1 indicates which sectors, on average, provide for the majority of undeclared hours worked, and if interviews carried out in 2004 and 2005 are regarded as one survey, and interviews carried out in 2006 are pooled with interviews carried out in 2007, we can compare results based on more even sample sizes and identical field periods.

Looking at three surveys—2001, 2004/2005, and 2006/2007—instead of five will "smooth out" the fluctuations and give a better overview but, obviously, does not remove the fluctuations or any underlying occasional underreporting or underestimation caused by other things. The overall conclusion is that, on average, the construction sector accounted for about one third of the total number of undeclared hours worked, followed by public and personal services and the primary sector both at about 10%. Financial intermediation and business activities, transport and telecommunications, sales and repairs, and hotels and restaurants all, on average, lie in the range 5 to less than 10%, while manufacturing shows a very constant level around 1%. It should be noted that because we only carried out one survey in 2007, these answers will have less weight than answers from twice as many interviews in 2006 when they are pooled.

As mentioned by way of introduction in this section, the distribution of undeclared activities may also be illustrated by looking at the number of hours worked without declaration as a proportion of the number of working hours in the formal part of the economy in each sector. This is done in Fig. 7.2.

In Fig. 7.2, undeclared hours worked as a proportion of declared hours tell more or less the same story as Fig. 7.1 did. The construction sector leads the sector groups with 13–14% on average for the whole period, but that figure is pulled slightly down by the unusually low 6½% in the two surveys carried out in 2006. Nevertheless, this means that 1 in every 10 hours worked in construction during the period covered by these surveys was undeclared, and significantly more in 2004 and 2007.

In spite of an overall decrease from 2001 to 2004 in the number of undeclared hours worked, the number of undeclared hours worked in construction increased. The economic recession in the official German economy at that time could mainly be attributed to the declining construction sector, and, in 2004–2005, one out of every five hours worked in the construction sector was done without declaration. The total number of hours worked in the formal part of the construction sector had decreased by about 20% in 2004–2005 compared with 2001 (Statistics Germany 2009, p. 84). At the same time, the undeclared part of construction hours increased by 15%, thus reducing the overall decline in (declared+undeclared) working hours in construction to 15–16%.

Since then the formal part of the economy has recovered and, according to Fig. 7.2, the undeclared part of construction has declined. However, the latter is ambiguous because of the low rates in 2006 which undeclared construction work clearly contributed to together with other of the more important sectors in this context like hotels and restaurants as well as transport. The last of the four most important sectors—the primary sector—developed differently from the other three, but it is an important observation that the decline in 2006 cannot be isolated to one single sector.

As far as the agriculture, fishing and quarrying group, which includes gardening as an important component, is concerned there are some remarkable outcomes: very few hours in 2004 and in 2007, but relatively many in 2006 in spite of a significant overall decline. It may be difficult to spot a possible trend when such fluctuations are at work, but undeclared hours' share of the total number of hours worked in the primary sector appears to have been declining slightly. The hotels and restaurants sector has experienced a similar development from 2001 to 2006, but in the single survey in 2007 the declining trend in this sector seems to have been reversed. However, this result is only tentative due to the relatively few interviews in 2007 and in the light of the fluctuations we have seen even when the sample sizes were larger. Undeclared hours' share of the total number of hours worked in this sector is, on average, about 5%—the same as in the transport and telecommunications sector. In other sectors, the number of undeclared hours' share is lower. In manufacturing the proportion is negligible.

Overall, the figures corroborate what is often heard of in the public discussion and in the media: undeclared work is concentrated in the construction sector, but the evidence is mixed when it comes to providing support—or the opposite—for the stated goal of the German Ministry of Finance to increase the personnel combating undeclared work (as well as other kinds of non-compliance) by enabling customs officials to investigate, in particular in the construction sector, on a broader scale. The total number of hours worked without declaration has declined compared with 2001, but the data for the important construction sector is ambiguous, and the results of the survey in 2007 indicate that the decrease in 2006 have been more than offset in 2007. However, due to the unusually low rate of participation in undeclared work in 2006, and due to the relatively few interviews in the 2007 survey, these results must be interpreted with care. Probably the agricultural sector and hotels and restaurants have become less important sectors for undeclared work, and it seems that the transport and telecommunications sector first gained in importance, then lost some again, and that it followed the general path of decline in 2006 and resumption in 2007.

7.4 Undeclared Work by Geographical Regions

Table 7.6 differentiates the proportions of individuals (18–66-year-olds) who carried out undeclared work and the number of undeclared working hours by the region they live in, giving figures for West and East Germany ("Früheres Bundesgebiet" and "Neue Länder"). While the proportions of undeclared activities were similar in 2001, with 11.4% in West and 12.7% in East Germany, a marked divergence has occurred since. In 2004, only 8.5% of the population carried out undeclared work in West Germany, while this figure was 13.9% in East Germany and undeclared work as a proportion of GDP even increased in East Germany in 2004. In 2005, the rate had increased to the same level as in 2001 in West Germany and increased further to 15.2% in East Germany. The dramatic decline in 2006 may be questioned but as shown in Table 7.6 it occurred in both East and West and rates also increased again in 2007 in both regions, but closer to the levels at the beginning of the period than to the levels found in 2005.

With respect to the average weekly number of undeclared hours worked by persons who carried out such activities, the numbers decreased for the West by about 1 h and remained virtually constant for the East from 2001 to 2004, meaning that the average for the whole population reflects the same divergence between West and East Germany as the frequency of carrying out undeclared work. West Germany experienced a similar decrease from 2004 to 2005 resulting in a decrease from about 8½ h in 2001 to 6¾ h in 2005. In East Germany the average undeclared

Table 7.6 Average number of undeclared working hours per week as a proportion of declared working hours, 18–66-year-olds, East and West Germany, 2001 and 2004–2007, in percent

	Frequency of doing undeclared work	Average undeclared working hours per week, persons who have carried out undeclared work	Average undeclared working hours per week, total population	Average normal declared working hours per week, total population[a]	Undeclared working hours as a proportion of declared hours ("percent of GDP")
	1	2	3 = (1×2)×100	4	5 = 3/4
	Proportion %	Hours per week[b]	Hours per week[b]	Hours per week[b]	Proportion %
2001					
West	11.4	8.58	0.98	24.0	4.08
East	12.7	7.33	0.93	21.9	4.25
Total	11.7	8.31	0.97	23.6	4.11
2004					
West	8.5	7.65	0.65	23.5	2.77
East	13.9	7.37	1.02	23.2	4.40
Total	9.6	7.56	0.73	23.4	3.12
2005					
West	11.4	6.78	0.77	23.8	3.24
East	15.2	6.84	1.04	21.7	4.79
Total	12.2	6.80	0.83	23.4	3.55
2006					
West	5.5	6.84	0.38	22.7	1.67
East	9.1	5.77	0.53	21.4	2.48
Total	6.3	6.52	0.41	22.4	1.83
2007					
West	10.2	5.73	0.58	20.8	2.79
East	12.6	7.75	0.98	22.5	4.36
Total	10.7	6.26	0.67	21.1	3.18

Source: The Rockwool Foundation Research unit's Shadow Economy Surveys

Note: The sample has been drawn at the household level, and a weight has been applied to make the sample representative as to gender and age distribution and other characteristics of the total population

[a]Number of hours worked in main and secondary jobs in the formal economy according to what is stated by the respondents in the surveys

[b]Minutes expressed as percentages of an hour

working week was reduced by about half an hour from 2004 to 2005 to 6 h 50 min. East and West both contributed to the decline in 2006, but there is a remarkable difference: while the respondents in East Germany reduced their average undeclared working week by about 1 h in 2006 and then subsequently increased it by 2 h to 7¾ h in 2007, respondents in West Germany maintained a constant undeclared working week in 2006 and then reduced it by 1 h to 5¾ h in 2007.

Similarly, undeclared hours as a proportion of declared working hours—a proxy for undeclared work at formal market prices as percent of GDP—remained between 4% and 5% in East, the exception being 2006, while the overall decreasing trend is due to the development in West Germany from just over 4% in 2001 to an average of approximately 3% when 2006 is disregarded. This is interesting because the results presented in Table 3.3 indicate higher tax morale in East Germany than in West Germany.

Table 7.7 (based on the 18–74-year-olds) underlines the findings of Table 7.6 by calculating the extent of undeclared activities based on actual prices paid in East and West respectively. While the extent of undeclared activities calculated at the actual prices prevailing in the shadow economy as a proportion of GDP (last column) was about 1¾ in East when 2006 is disregarded, fluctuations can be attributed to the conduct of people living in West Germany. In rounded figures, the actual pricing of undeclared work in West Germany gives them a monetary value corresponding to between 0.9% and 1.4% of GDP when the exceptionally low level of 0.59% in 2006 is disregarded. As can also be seen from Table 7.7, it is not only variations in the number of hours worked in the shadow economy in West Germany that influences the overall picture, variations in prices and wages do the same. The average hourly remuneration in West increased from about 11 Euros at the beginning of the period to 15 Euros in 2005 and then decreased slightly to 13–14 Euros in 2006–2007. It is interesting to notice that prices and wages paid in the East are significantly lower at 8–9 Euros, the exception being the single wave of interviews in 2007 where the average payment is slightly higher at 9.7 Euros.

Undeclared work thus seems to have kept its importance in East Germany, whereas its importance appears to have decreased in West Germany. The decrease in West is attributable rather to the number of hours worked by the people involved than to the number of people involved as such.

7.5 Summarizing the Main Findings

Summarizing the findings from Chap. 7, it must be emphasized again that estimates of the extent of undeclared work which are based on the survey method can only provide a lower limit of the actual size of this part of the shadow economy. Overall, the size of the undeclared sector decreased from 4.1% relative to official GDP in 2001 to 3.1% in 2004 measured as the total number of hours worked without declaration as a proportion of the total number of working hours on the formal labor market. Even though the participation rate increased to the highest level measured in these surveys in 2005, undeclared work "only" reached 3.6% measured as a percentage of declared working hours ("percent of GDP"), because average undeclared weekly working hours continued to decrease. After a drop to 1.83% in 2006, a participation rate of 10.7% among (here) the 18–66-year-olds (as the comparison is with working hours on the formal labor market) combined with an average undeclared working week of now just over 6¼ h resulted in an undeclared sector which amounted to 3.18% relative to GDP in 2007. Given the unusually low and not very plausible participation rate in 2006, we will not put too much emphasis on the 1.83%.

Table 7.7 Extent of undeclared work based on actual prices paid, 18–74-year-olds, East and West Germany, 2001 and 2004–2007

	Number of undeclared working hours per year Million hours[b,c]	Average hourly wage for undeclared work Euro (current prices)[d]	Extent of undeclared work at actual prices paid Million Euros (current prices)[c,d]	Extent of undeclared work at actual prices paid as a proportion of GDP[a] %
2001				
West	2,177	10.7	23,294	1.27
East	530	8.7	4,611	1.64
Total	2,707	10.3	27,882	1.32
2004				
West	1,531	11.1	16,994	0.89
East	588	8.7	5,116	1.74
Total	2,096	10.4	21,798	0.99
2005				
West	1,752	15.1	26	1.36
East	596	8.8	5,245	1.76
Total	2,353	13.3	31,295	1.40
2006				
West	886	13.5	11,961	0.59
East	304	7.9	2,402	0.78
Total	1,184	11.8	13,971	0.60
2007				
West	1,344	14.2	19,085	0.91
East	574	9.7	5,568	1.73
Total	1,935	13.0	25,155	1.04

Source: The Rockwool Foundation Research Unit's Shadow Economy Surveys

[a]GDP (million Euros) from Eurostat's homepage http://epp.eurostat.ec.europa.eu (Data—Economy and finance—National accounts (including GDP)): 2001: 2.113.160, 2004: 2.210.900, 2005: 2.243.200, 2006: 2.321.500, 2007: 2.422.900. East (Neue Länder including half of Berlin's GDP) and West German (Früheres Bundesgebiet including the other half of Berlin's GDP) proportions of GDP of 13.3% and 86.7% respectively are based on the proportions in 2001–2006 according to Statistics Germany (2007, p. 653)

[b]Frequency of doing undeclared work/100 × average number of undeclared working hours per week by persons who have carried out undeclared work × 52 × total population aged 18–74 on 1 January. Population, 18–74 years, from Eurostat's homepage http://epp.eurostat.ec.europa.eu (Data—Population and social conditions—Population): 2001: 60.825.462, 2004: 61.090.674, 2005: 61.107.853, 2006: 61.144.646, 2007: 61.204.638. According to Statistics Germany (2007, pp. 34–35) between 20% and 21% of all Germans live in East Germany. In Table 7.6, the proportions according to the surveys, which vary between 19.7% and 20.8%, have been used

[c]Due to rounding "Total" can be different from the total of East and West

[d]The monthly incomes in DEM in 2001 have been converted to Euro by using the synthetic average exchange rate for 2001

Calculating the extent of undeclared work by using the actual hourly wages prevailing in that part of the economy instead, which, by definition, are lower than the official market price implicitly assumed in the above calculation, leads to a decrease from 1.35% in 2001 to 1.0% in 2004 which, however, was more than offset in 2005 when the proportion reached about 1.4%. The lowest level—0.6%—is again found in 2006, but, as mentioned, an important question to investigate is how much of this decrease is actually due to changes in the level of participation in undeclared activities and how much is caused by other things. In 2007, undeclared working hours times actual prices paid for undeclared work corresponded to 1% of the official GDP.

The "potential" for undeclared work, which is the proportion who either had carried out undeclared work during the last 12 months or would, in principle, be willing to do so, also decreased, but only slightly, from 25.5% in 2001 to 24.4% in 2004, then increased to 28.6% in 2005, dropped to 20.3% in 2006 and increased to 26.0% in 2007—the same level as in 2001.

A third way to illustrate the extent of undeclared work is to "convert" the number of hours worked without declaration per year to full-time jobs. Had all undeclared hours worked in 2001 been transferred to the formal economy, it would have corresponded to 1.63 million full-time jobs. Obviously, not all undeclared activities can automatically be transferred to the formal market, but if one third could be converted to work in the formal economy, it would still amount to more than 500,000 jobs. In 2004, undeclared work corresponded to 1.25 million full-time jobs (one third of which amounts to about 420,000 jobs). In 2005, 2006, and 2007, similar calculations result in 1.40 million (465,000), 0.71 million (235,000), and 1.15 million (385,000) jobs respectively.

Even though decreases have been followed by increases every second year, the estimates of the total number of undeclared hours, as well as the monetary evaluation of these activities, seem to indicate a slightly downward trend in the extent of undeclared work in Germany because decreases have not been fully offset the year after. The downward trend is due primarily to a continuously reduced average number of hours spent on undeclared work by people engaged in such activities.

In addition, the structural results are very interesting. This first relates to the structure of undeclared work by sector. The average for the whole period places about one third of the hours worked without declaration in construction while public and personal services and the primary sector (agriculture etc. including gardening) both account for about 10%. Financial intermediation and business activities, transport and telecommunications, sales and repairs, and hotels and restaurants all, on average, lie in the range 5 to less than 10%, while manufacturing shows a very constant level around 1%.

The distribution of undeclared activities may also be illustrated by looking at the number of hours worked without declaration as a proportion of the number of working hours in the formal part of the economy in each sector. Such calculations also, on average, found the largest proportion in the construction sector. Over the period as a whole including the ambiguous results in 2006, about 1 in every 10 hours worked in construction was undeclared. As an illustration we showed that while the total number of hours worked in the formal part of the construction sector had decreased by about 20% in 2004–2005 compared with 2001, the undeclared part of construction work measured in hours increased by 15%, thus reducing the overall decline in (declared + undeclared) working hours in construction to 15–16%.

It is difficult to spot a clear picture for the second most important group, the primary sector which includes gardening as an important component, because of some large fluctuations, but undeclared hours' share of the total number of hours worked appears to have been declining slightly. Undeclared hours' share of the total number of hours worked in the hotels and restaurants sector is, on average, about 5% as in the transport and telecommunications sector. In other sectors proportions are lower. In manufacturing the proportion is negligible.

Finally, the amounts of undeclared work among people living in West and East Germany respectively were relatively close in 2001 but a marked divergence has occurred since then. Undeclared hours as a proportion of declared working hours, which we use as a proxy for undeclared work at formal market prices as percent of GDP, remained between 4% and 5% in the East, the exception being 2006, while the overall decreasing trend is due to the development in West Germany from just over 4% in 2001 to an average of approximately 3% when 2006 is disregarded.

While the extent of undeclared activities calculated at the actual prices prevailing in the shadow economy as a proportion of GDP was about 1¾ in East except in 2006, fluctuations can be attributed to the conduct of people living in West Germany. In rounded figures, the actual pricing of undeclared work in West Germany gives them a monetary value corresponding to between 0.9 and 1.4% of GDP (0.59% in 2006). This is not only due to variations in the number of hours worked in the shadow economy in West Germany but also to variations in prices and wages paid. The average hourly remuneration in the West increased from about 11 Euros at the beginning of the period to 15 Euros in 2005 and then decreased slightly to 13–14 Euros in 2006–2007. The prices and wages paid in East Germany are significantly lower: 8–9 Euros except in the single wave of interviews in 2007 where the average payment is slightly higher—but still 4.5 Euros below the average in West Germany.

Undeclared work thus seems to have kept its importance in East Germany, whereas its importance appears to have decreased in West Germany. The decrease in West Germany is attributable more to the number of hours worked by the people involved than to the number of people involved as such.

These results are interesting both in the light of the continuous campaigns against undeclared work (and other kinds of tax evasion) and given the results presented in Chap. 3 which indicate higher tax morale in East as compared to West Germany.

Chapter 8
The Impact of Deterrence on Undeclared Work

Given the mainly descriptive evidence in the previous chapters, the most important question is whether a policy of deterrence is actually a suitable means with which to fight undeclared work in Germany. The German Federal government and in particular the German Finance Ministry is convinced of the effectiveness of such policies. As outlined in the introduction and in Chap. 4, deterrence has increased across time in Germany. A whole sequence of steps has been carried out in order to raise deterrence levels considerably. Such initiatives are founded on economic theory according to which the risk of sanctions and the size of fines are expected to have a significant impact on tax evasion and thereby also undeclared work. In this chapter we look into whether this is the case.

The literature on this topic originates from Becker's (1968) economic theory of crime and the economic model of tax evasion which subsequently was derived by Allingham and Sandmo (1972). According to this line of thinking, tax evasion can be analyzed by focusing on its costs and benefits to the individual who evades. The benefits depend on the individual's marginal tax rate and true income. The costs of tax evasion depend on the level of deterrence, i.e. the risk of detection and the sanction in the form of a fine or imprisonment. A fine thus functions like a price (Gneezy and Rustichini 2000) and if the price (the fine) increases then people will be less willing to buy (evade). They substitute activities in the formal sector of the economy for those in the informal sector.

We will put words like "expected" and "perceived" before benefits and sanctions etc. because we all act on what we subjectively believe to be the facts. Taxpayers' calculations thus are based on *subjective* probabilities of being detected and punished should they decide to cheat and try to evade taxes. Furthermore, the outcome of such a cost-benefit calculation crucially depends on the "risk preferences" of the individual taxpayer: the more risk-averse a person is, the larger the difference must be between, on the one hand, the perceived probability (chance) of getting away with cheating multiplied by the expected gain and, on the other hand, the perceived probability (risk) of being detected if cheating multiplied by the monetary evaluation of the sanction.

L.P. Feld and C. Larsen, *Undeclared Work, Deterrence and Social Norms*,
DOI 10.1007/978-3-540-87401-0_8, © Springer-Verlag Berlin Heidelberg 2012

Even though a deterrence policy is well in line with orthodox economic thinking, both subjectively perceived probabilities and risk preferences as well as individual tax morale and other social norms, among other things, provide challenges for the purely economic approach as there will inevitably be misperceptions and neither individual risk preferences nor social norms are immediately observable. After all, the matter of the impact of deterrence on tax evasion is an empirical issue, and the international evidence available is not fully convincing, but rather mixed and ambiguous. As mentioned in the introduction, there may even be a crowding out of tax compliance when penalties are introduced like Scholz and Lubell (2001) find. Feld and Frey (2002a) provide support for the ambiguous impact of deterrence on tax compliance. For a panel of Swiss cantons, they find that greater intensity of control increases tax evasion, while fines and penalties reduce tax evasion.

Although the overall decline in undeclared work between 2001 and 2004 coincided with increases in deterrence, and although surveys carried out after 2004 suggest that if not the number of participants in the shadow economy then at least the total amount of hours they spent on undeclared work has declined, this decline could be the result of other variables which have not been controlled for. For example, the tax and labor market reform acts in Germany could equally well have contributed to the reductions in the extent of undeclared work. Tax policy is the subject of Chap. 9, while tax morale (and other social norms) is the subject of Chap. 10.

8.1 Measuring Deterrence in the Survey

Deterrence has two components: the probability of detection and the size of fines. Given the design of our study, it is not possible to estimate the impact of changes in objective deterrence on the extent of undeclared work. Because our survey provides individual data, it is possible to get information on subjectively perceived deterrence only. In 2011, this issue was not fully addressed as questions on fines and sanctions were not posed. In both 2001 and in 2004–2007, questions were asked about the perceived risk of detection:

> People who carry out ‘undeclared work’ risk the authorities finding out and issuing supplementary tax bills and perhaps fines, etc. In your opinion, what level of risk do people who carry out ‘undeclared work’ run? Is it very high, fairly high, fairly small, or very small?

The answers are shown in Table 8.1.

According to these figures, a rather large proportion of the population thought that the risk was very high or fairly high. Although the proportion of respondents assessing the probability of detection as very high declined from 10.8% in 2001 to 9.4% in 2004, the proportion who perceived the risk of being caught as fairly high increased from 25.4% in 2001 to 29.7% in 2004 and in the interviews carried out during the period 2005–2007 more than 40% assessed the risk as fairly high or very high. Moreover, the number of individuals making a low assessment of the risk

Table 8.1 Perceived risk of being detected and punished for carrying out undeclared work, 18–74-year-olds, Germany, 2001 and 2004–2007, in percent

	Very high	Fairly high	Fairly small	Very small	Don't know/refusal	Total	No. of persons
2001	10.8	25.4	30.1	18.2	15.6	100	5,686
2004	9.4	29.7	32.3	15.1	13.5	100	2,143
2005	11.5	31.3	32.4	13.8	11.1	100	2,144
2006	11.7	30.3	30.9	16.3	10.9	100	2,176
2007	12.0	28.7	34.8	12.6	12.0	100	1,096

Source: The Rockwool Foundation Research Unit's Shadow Economy Surveys
Note: The sample has been drawn at the household level, and a weight has been applied to make the sample representative as to gender and age distribution and other characteristics of the total population. The number of persons shown in the table is the actual number before the weight was applied

declined, as did the item non-response rate. The policy measures implemented since 2001 and the campaigns accompanying these measures appear to have had an impact on individual perceptions.

The 2001 survey did not, however, include any questions about the perceived sanctions for carrying out undeclared work, size of fines or risk of imprisonment. Thus, an additional question was included in the survey in 2004 about the perceived sanctions:

> If the authorities find out that somebody has carried out 'undeclared work', the taxes due must be paid and perhaps the person will also become liable to fine or imprisonment. In your opinion, what sanction is to be expected if the authorities find out that somebody has carried out 'undeclared work' to the value of 2,500 Euros?

In 2006, it was supplemented by a similar question involving undeclared work to the value of 10,000 Euros. The answers are shown in Table 8.2.

Respondents could choose from four different discrete alternatives. The first was that people caught doing undeclared work would only be required to pay the taxes due. When the question was about undeclared work to the value of 2,500 Euros, about 20% of the respondents in our surveys had this perception in 2004 but the share has increased and peaked in 2006 at 28.1%. It may therefore seem counterintuitive that the lowest rate of participation in undeclared work also was found in 2006. In 2004 and 2005, more than half chose the second option which adds a fine to the payment of the taxes due, while the proportion which chose this category decreased by about 10 percentage points in 2006, but then increased again to just over 50% in 2007. The second option appears to be relatively realistic, given the discussion in Chap. 4.

In 2006 and 2007, the second option was divided into two to make it possible for the respondents to report their assessment of the *size* of the fine as well. In 2004 and 2005, respondents could also infer that a prison sentence would be imposed in addition to paying the taxes evaded and/or a fine. In 2004 and 2005, a total of only 4.9% and 7.8% of respondents chose this option, which was not included in the following surveys in 2006 and 2007. Almost a quarter of the respondents did not assess the sanction, the exception being the survey in 2005 where the proportion of respondents in this category was halved.

Table 8.2 Expected sanction if a person has carried out undeclared work to the value of 2,500 Euros or to the value of 10,000 Euros, 18–74-year-olds, Germany, 2004–2007, in percent

	Taxes due must be paid	Taxes due and a fine of 50–100% of taxes due must be paid[a]	Taxes due and a fine of 150–200% or more of taxes due must be paid[a]	Imprisonment[b]	Don't know/ refusal	Total	No. of persons
	... to the value of 2,500 Euros						
2004	19.9	51.2		4.9	24.0	100	2,143
2005	26.3	53.5		7.8	12.4	100	2,144
2006	28.1	29.9	14.2	–	27.8	100	2,176
2007	24.2	36.8	13.9	–	25.2	100	1,096
	... to the value of 10,000 Euros[c]						
2006	10.5	23.4	25.3	11.6	29.2	100	2,176
2007	10.4	22.1	32.4	10.7	24.5	100	1,096

Source: The Rockwool Foundation Research Unit's Shadow Economy Surveys

Note: The sample has been drawn at the household level, and a weight has been applied to make the sample representative as to gender and age distribution and other characteristics of the total population. The number of persons shown in the table is the actual number before the weight was applied

[a]In 2004–2005, the size of fines was not specified

[b]In the interviews carried out in August 2004, the respondents could choose between two answer categories which included imprisonment: (1) taxes due must be paid and imprisonment and (2) taxes due and a fine must be paid and imprisonment, whereas in October 2004 and in April and June 2005, there was only one category involving imprisonment: (2) taxes due and a fine must be paid and imprisonment. In 2006–2007, imprisonment was not included as a possible answer category when the question was about undeclared work to the value of 2,500 Euros

[c]The question about undeclared work to the value of 10,000 Euros was not asked in 2004–2005

Turning to the question about the perceived punishment for carrying out undeclared work to the value of 10,000 Euros, which was only asked in 2006 and 2007, and where imprisonment was only a possible answer when the amount was 10,000 Euros, between a quarter and close to 30% of the respondents did not assess the sanction. About 10% chose the first option, i.e. taxes due must be paid, and a similar number of the respondents opted for the most severe punishment, i.e. imprisonment. In 2006, one quarter of the respondents assessed that in addition to paying the taxes due, a fine of 50–100% of the taxes due would have to be paid. Another quarter of the respondents assessed that the fine would be higher. In 2007, the latter assessment was shared by 32.4% of the respondents against 22.1 who opted for the lower fine. This does not indicate an increase in the perceived sanction for undeclared work.

8.2 Perceived Risk and Sanctions by Geographical Regions

A differentiation according to region like in Chap. 7 does not reveal any significant differences between East and West Germany when it comes to the perceived risk of being detected and punished by the authorities for carrying out undeclared work (see Table 8.3).

Table 8.3 Perceived risk of being detected and punished for carrying out undeclared work, 18–74-year-olds, East and West Germany, 2001 and 2004–2007, in percent

	Very high	Fairly high	Fairly small	Very small	Don't know/refusal	Total	No. of persons
2001 West	10.4	25.5	30.0	18.5	15.6	100	4,552
East	12.5	24.7	30.2	17.1	15.6	100	1,134
2004 West	9.6	29.5	33.4	14.4	13.2	100	1,766
East	8.7	30.7	28.0	17.7	14.9	100	377
2005 West	10.5	31.4	32.7	14.2	11.3	100	1,677
East	15.7	30.7	31.4	12.3	10.0	100	467
2006 West	10.8	29.9	31.1	16.2	12.1	100	1,726
East	15.2	32.1	29.8	17.1	6.0	100	450
2007 West	12.4	27.7	36.6	11.9	11.5	100	859
East	10.5	32.5	27.9	15.5	13.8	100	237

Source: The Rockwool Foundation Research Unit's Shadow Economy Surveys
Note: The sample has been drawn at the household level, and a weight has been applied to make the sample representative as to gender and age distribution and other characteristics of the total population. The number of persons shown in the table is the actual number before the weight was applied

In Table 8.4, we show the answers to the two questions about expected sanctions for doing undeclared work. The two regions do not differ systematically from each other as far as the answer categories involving only payment of taxes due and fines are concerned, but there seems to be a tendency for respondents from East Germany to expect imprisonment more often than respondents from West Germany do, in particular when the question is about undeclared work to the value of 10,000 Euros.

In the next section we enter the deterrence variables introduced in this section—perceived risk and perceived sanction—into a regression analysis to see how they correlate with participation in undeclared work. It should be stressed that a regression analysis does not necessarily establish causal relationships between the dependent variable (here: undeclared work) and the explanatory variables (here: socio-economic factors and deterrence)—merely correlations.

8.3 An Econometric Analysis of Deterrence and Undeclared Work

8.3.1 Perceived Risk of Detection

In order to obtain more systematic evidence on the possible impact of deterrence on the probability of carrying out undeclared work, we follow the same approach as in Chap. 6. Again, a logistic regression is performed and in Table 8.5, the model estimated and discussed in Chap. 6 is extended with a variable which captures deterrence by including the perceived risk of being caught. The detailed regression results are shown in Appendix Table 8. As can be seen, this variable negatively affects the probability of participating in undeclared work if the *perceived risk of*

Table 8.4 Expected sanction if a person has carried out undeclared work to the value of 2,500 Euros or to the value of 10,000 Euros, 18–74-year-olds, East and West Germany, 2004–2007, in percent

	Taxes due must be paid	Taxes due and a fine of 50–100% of taxes due must be paid[a]	Taxes due and a fine of 150–200% or more of taxes due must be paid[a]	Imprisonment[b]	Don't know/ refusal	Total	No. of persons
	… to the value of 2,500 Euros						
2004 West	20.1	53.4		4.7	21.7	100	1,766
East	19.0	42.5		5.6	32.9	100	377
2005 West	26.7	54.1		7.3	11.9	100	1,677
East	24.6	51.3		9.8	14.3	100	467
2006 West	26.8	29.7	14.1	–	29.5	100	1,726
East	33.2	30.8	14.6	–	21.5	100	450
2007 West	23.7	38.5	13.0	–	24.8	100	859
East	25.8	30.4	17.4	–	26.4	100	237
	… to the value of 10,000 Euros[c]						
2006 West	10.0	24.8	24.2	10.3	30.7	100	1,726
East	12.8	17.8	29.6	16.2	23.5	100	450
2007 West	10.5	21.4	34.4	9.0	24.6	100	859
East	9.7	24.7	24.9	17.0	23.8	100	237

Source: The Rockwool Foundation Research Unit's Shadow Economy Surveys

Note: The sample has been drawn at the household level, and a weight has been applied to make the sample representative as to gender and age distribution and other characteristics of the total population. The number of persons shown in the table is the actual number before the weight was applied

[a]In 2004–2005, the size of fines was not specified

[b]In the interviews carried out in August 2004, the respondents could choose between two answer categories which included imprisonment: (1) taxes due must be paid and imprisonment and (2) taxes due *and* a fine must be paid and imprisonment, whereas in October 2004 and in April and June 2005, there was only one category involving imprisonment: (2) taxes due *and* a fine must be paid and imprisonment. In 2006–2007, imprisonment was not included as a possible answer category when the question was about undeclared work to the value of 2,500 Euros

[c]The question about undeclared work to the value of 10,000 Euros was not asked in 2004–2005

detection is very high or fairly high, and this effect is highly significant for women as well as for men.

This variable stays significant when 2001 is omitted and the regressions are performed on the basis of a pooled data set (2004–2007 or 2004–2008), although it is not significant every year, and in 2006 it is only significant when missing values are treated as a separate answer category, not when missing values are set to the median value of the answers from the rest of the respondents. In joint regressions for men and women, risk is highly significant.

Variables which were significant at least at the 5% level in Table 6.3 remain significant in Table 8.5. That means that *age* correlates as expected with the propensity to carry out undeclared work for men and the effect now even becomes significant, but at a low level, for the 50–59-year-old men. Age does not have the same

Table 8.5 Logistic regression of the probability of participating in undeclared work, 18–74-year-olds, 2001 and 2004–2007

	Men	Women
Age	√	(√)
Marital status	–	√
Children under 6	–	–
Occupation	√	√
Education	√	–
Respondent's monthly net income	√	√
Length of unemployment	√	–
Region (East/West Germany)	–	–
Owner-occupied/not owner-occupied home	–	–
Year the survey was carried out	√	√
Perceived risk of detection	√	√

Source: The Rockwool Foundation Research Unit's Shadow Economy Surveys
Note: √: significant effect at least at the 5% level, (√): significant effect but only at the 10% level, –: not significant. Details are shown in Appendix Table 8. The sample has been drawn at the household level, and a weight has been applied to make the sample representative as to gender and age distribution and other characteristics of the total population

importance for women, while the situation is the opposite as far as *marital status* is concerned. Married women are much less likely to have carried out undeclared work than single women while it is not of any importance in the regression for men, even though the sign is the same, i.e. negative, except in the regressions based on the data collected in 2004. In joint regressions for men and women, marital status is highly significant regardless of how many of the qualitative explaining variables we add.

As to *occupation*, skilled men and women have a relatively high probability of having answered in the affirmative. This effect even becomes more significant for men when the perceived risk is included in the regression analysis, but, as already mentioned in Sect. 6.2 and shown in the next section, this variable loses its significance when the data from 2001 is omitted. Also unskilled women and female students remain more likely than the reference group (salaried workers) to have carried out undeclared work with risk included. A Fachschule *education* remains significant with a positive sign for men, while men without any education or training qualifying for the labor market are less likely to have answered yes, but the latter effect is only significant at a low level. As we show in Chap. 10, where we use the largest possible data set in a joint regression for men and women with all variables included, Fachschule is significant, though less so when the survey from 2008 is added to the data set, as well as skilled and unskilled workers, though not so significant as Fachschule and not significant when 2008 is added.

Respondents with a *monthly net income* below 1,000 Euros are more likely to have answered yes than persons with higher income, though this effect has lost a bit of its significance for women. However, like occupation, income is also a factor which owes its significance to 2001. Finally, for men who are out of work the probability increases with the period of *unemployment*. This effect is unchanged compared with Chap. 6.

As far as the *year of the interview* is concerned, 2006 still is the only significant year for men, but as stressed earlier this result does not imply much. Ignoring 2006, one cannot reject the hypothesis that the participation rate is unchanged for men during the whole period. The picture is different for women, as each year differs significantly from the reference year (2001) in this regression. Compared with the previous regression in Table 6.3, the negative effect on the probability of participation in undeclared work of interviews carried out in 2006 or in 2007 becomes a little less significant, while the positive effect from interviews carried out in 2005 now becomes significant, but only at the 10% level, and the negative effect from interviews carried out in 2004 remains significant at the same low (10%) level.

8.3.2 Perceived Sanction If Detected

The probability—or rather risk—of detection is only a part of deterrence; the full effect of deterrence must capture the sanction as well. Therefore, we now include the categories measuring the perceived sanction as summarized in Table 8.2 in the logistic regression. The category "Taxes due must be paid", i.e. the lowest possible sanction, is left out of the regression to avoid perfect collinearity. The effects of the other two, and more severe, categories of punishment are thus measured relative to "Taxes due must be paid", and a negative sign for these other categories could be expected with increasing coefficients, if the respondents believe that it is realistic that such sanctions will actually be enforced. Table 8.6 summarizes the findings of the more detailed regression results from Appendix Table 9.

Table 8.6 Logistic regression of the probability of participating in undeclared work, 18–74-year-olds, Germany, 2004–2007

	Men	Women
Age	√	(√)
Marital status	–	√
Children under 6	–	–
Occupation	–	(√)
Education	(√)	–
Respondent's monthly net income	–	–
Length of unemployment	(√)	–
Region (East/West Germany)	(√)	–
Owner-occupied/not owner-occupied home	–	–
Year the survey was carried out	√	√
Perceived risk of detection	√	√
Perceived sanction if detected	–	–

Source: The Rockwool Foundation Research Unit's Shadow Economy Surveys
Note: √: significant effect at least at the 5% level, (√): significant effect but only at the 10% level, –: not significant. Details are shown in Appendix Table 9. The sample has been drawn at the household level, and a weight has been applied to make the sample representative as to gender and age distribution and other characteristics of the total population

Because questions about the perceived sanctions for having carried out undeclared work, and thus evaded tax and social security payments and possibly neglected other obligations as well, were not included in the survey in 2001 we will have to perform this and the rest of the regressions without the data collected for that year. Furthermore, as explained in Sects. 8.1 and 8.2, the way of asking these questions was adjusted several times from 2004 to 2006. The latest version of the question is always used in the regressions. Therefore, in 2004 and 2005, the amount of evasion involved is 2,500 Euros while it is 10,000 Euros in 2006 and 2007. This may complicate the interpretation of the results to some extent, and the fact that as many as 25–30% of the respondents did not answer the questions about the size of sanctions also complicates the analysis. In the regressions, respondents with missing values have—as a starting point—been given the median value of the other respondents' answers. The results were compared with the results of parallel regressions where an extra dummy variable was added to capture the effect of not answering the question.

As can be seen from Table 8.6, one consequence of adding perceived sanction as an explanatory variable—and thereby excluding the 5,686 interviews carried out in 2001 where this and the questions which are the topics of the next two chapters were not asked—is a decrease in the number of significant effects and significance levels. We have not shown the results of the pooled regressions with only socio-economic variables and with socio-economic variables and risk included based on 2004–2007 because the inclusion of new variables to evaluate the effect of perceived sanctions for tax evasion etc. in connection with undeclared work does not change anything significantly as far as the existing variables are concerned.

One thing that pulls in the opposite direction of decreasing significance is that *region* now becomes significant for men: the probability of answering yes is lower among men living in West Germany than among men living in East Germany. However, the significance level is highest in the regression with only socio-economic variables included—almost exactly 7.5%—and it gradually decreases to disappear again when social norms are included in Chap. 10. However, region is an area where it plays a role, whether the pooled regressions are based on 2004–2007 or on 2004–2008, as the interviews which were carried out in 2008 showed a particularly significant difference between respondents living in the Eastern parts of the country and respondents living in the Western parts. As shown in Chaps. 3 and 7, the participation rates developed in different directions in East and West, and this tendency actually was intensified in 2008 (16% and 8% respectively among the 18–74-year-olds which may be compared with the figures in Table 3.2 for 2001 and 2004–2007).

In this specification of the model, the perceived *sanction* does not appear to be important when a person decides whether or not to engage in undeclared work. Appendix Table 9 shows that the signs are as one would expect, i.e. negative as we are comparing two more threatening alternatives with the least serious sanction, but the effects are not significant. Another consequence of not being able to use the data from 2001 is that the effect of the perceived *risk* of detection becomes less significant in the regressions for men. It is not important for the significance level of the effect of risk whether sanction is included or not. In regressions performed for each year separately, perceived sanction actually is significant and with the expected sign for men in 2005 and in 2007. The effect is significant at the 10% level in 2005 and highly significant in 2007. Sanction is also significant in 2006 and this time for both men and women, but with the opposite sign so respondents expecting a more severe sanction than just having to pay the taxes due have a higher probability of having participated in an undeclared job—ceteris paribus—than the reference group "Taxes due must be paid". In a joint regression with men and women and data from 2004 to 2008, the effect of missings in this variable is significant at the 10% level and negative, but it becomes insignificant, when marginal tax is added as an explanatory variable, and it stays insignificant when norms are added.

In short, so far the estimation results based on data from 2004 to 2007 indicate that *age* plays a role: young men in the age group 18–29 years have a highly significant probability of having carried out undeclared work during the last 12 months. Men and women aged 60–74 years have a relatively low probability. In both cases the reference group is the 40–49-year-olds and all other things are being kept equal. An equally very robust effect as that young men work undeclared is that *married* women do not.

As to *occupation* and *education*, a higher probability is found among unskilled women compared with the reference group (salaried workers) and among men with a Fachschule education compared with the reference group (beruflich-betriebliche Ausbildung). Furthermore, *length of unemployment* is significant and positive for the probability among men while *region* has the effect of reducing the probability for those living in West Germany, but also only for men.

Ignoring the ambiguous results from the interviews carried out in 2006, the *timing of the interviews* does not result in significantly different probabilities of participation as far as men are concerned. Among women, the interviews carried out in 2005 result in a highly significant and significantly higher probability compared with the reference year (2004), while the interviews carried out in 2006 or in 2007 do not differ significantly from the reference year.

The perceived *risk of detection* appears to have a strong effect among women and a relatively strong effect among men—in both cases with the expected (negative) sign (when respondents who perceive the risk to be high are compared with respondents who perceive the risk to be low). Finally, the variables measuring the perceived *punishment* for evasion of tax and social security payments connected with undeclared work also have the expected signs but they do not reach any conventional significance level.

8.4 Summarizing the Main Findings

The efforts to fight undeclared work and other forms of tax evasion through deterrence measures have increased in Germany during the period which the interviews in this study cover. The German Federal government and in particular the German Finance Ministry is convinced of the effectiveness of such a policy and this policy is founded on economic theory.

In this chapter we have looked into the impact of deterrence on undeclared work by introducing qualitative variables to capture the individually perceived risk and level of sanctions in connection with undeclared work.

A rather large proportion of the population considered the risk to be very high or fairly high. The proportion increased from a total of approximately 36% in 2001 to 39% in 2004 and to more than 40% in 2005–2007. The policy measures implemented since 2001 and the campaigns accompanying these measures thus appear to have had an impact on individual perceptions.

Questions about the perceived sanctions were not asked until 2004. Furthermore, the way of asking was adjusted a couple of times between 2004 and 2006 and as many as 25–30% of the respondents did not answer the questions about sanctions. This may complicate the interpretation of this variable to some extent, but at first glance the descriptive evidence does not indicate an increase in the perceived level of sanctions for undeclared work.

When the question was asked for the first time in 2004, it was about undeclared work to the value of 2,500 Euros. In 2006, a question was added where the amount was raised to 10,000 Euros. When the question is about 2,500 Euros, 20–28% of the respondents answered that the only sanction would be that the taxes due would have to be paid, while 5–8% thought that the sanction would be prison. Prison as an option was removed in 2006 and instead the second option which adds a fine to the payment of the taxes due was split up in two. Overall, about half of the respondents chose the second option which also appears to be relatively realistic. When it became possible to differentiate, 30–37% opted for a fine of 50–100% of the taxes due while 14% opted for a fine of 100–200%. When the question is about 10,000 Euros, 10–11% thought that the only consequence in case of detection would be that taxes due would have to be paid, while 11–12% thought that the sanction would include imprisonment. About half of the respondents chose a fine.

A differentiation according to region does not reveal any systematic differences between East and West Germany except that there seems to be a tendency for respondents from East Germany to expect imprisonment more often than respondents from West Germany do, in particular when the question is about undeclared work to the value of 10,000 Euros.

When the first of the deterrence variables—risk—is entered into a regression analysis to see how it correlates with participation in undeclared work, we find that if the risk of detection is perceived as being very high or fairly high it has a negative affect on the probability of having carried out undeclared work, and this effect is highly significant for women as well as for men. Variables which were significant at least at the 5% level in the regression in Chap. 6 where only socio-economic variables were included remain significant when risk is included.

When sanctions are included in order to capture the full effect of deterrence, data from 2001 has to be omitted, because such questions were not asked until 2004. One consequence of this is a decrease in the number of significant effects and in the level of significance compared with the regressions with 2001 included, e.g., the effect of risk loses significance for men. This is an effect of omitting data from 2001, not an effect of including sanctions. Omitting data from 2001 also makes region significant for men—but only at a low level—so those who live in West Germany have a lower probability of answering yes than those who live in East Germany.

The perceived risk of detection appears to have a strong effect among women and a relatively strong effect among men and in both cases with the expected (negative) sign when respondents who perceive the risk to be high are compared with respondents who perceive the risk to be low. The effects of the perceived level of sanctions for evasion of tax and social security payments connected with undeclared work do not reach any conventional significance level, although they have the expected signs, too. It is not surprising that sanctions are not significant in particular when compared with the perceived risk of being detected. Within a single year the variation of perceived sanctions across individuals in our samples is only obtained from their perceptions (or misperceptions). In 1 year observed, there is no external variance like a policy change in fines and sanctions induced by the government. In contrast, the perceived risk of being detected in one single year may also be influenced by experiences of actual controls by the tax authorities that an individual could have made in his peer group or on his own. Thus, this evidence at least partly appears to be in favor of the hypothesis that deterrence is the policy of choice for a fight against undeclared work.

Chapter 9
The Impact of Tax Policy on Undeclared Work

According to the economic theory of tax evasion, the extent of undeclared work could also – in addition to deterrence – be affected by either tax policies or tax morale. The possibility has already been mentioned that the German tax reform act of 2000, which has been implemented in stages up until 2005, could have affected the pattern of undeclared activities between 2001 and 2004. And when the tax reform was fully implemented in 2005, income taxes in Germany had been cut considerably from a marginal tax rate going from 22.9% for the lowest taxable income bracket to 51% for the highest income bracket in the year 2000 to 15% and 42% respectively. Taxpayers have to pay the solidarity surcharge and social security contributions, both of which increase the tax burden on labor income, but nevertheless the overall reduction in income taxes has been considerable in the recent past.

There is some evidence to be found in the literature about the impact of tax policy on tax compliance (Feld and Frey 2007). Most studies find a positive impact of marginal tax rates on tax evasion or the size of the shadow economy, though this evidence is not uncontested. Theoretically, a negative or positive sign for the marginal tax rate can be expected, depending on how progressive the income tax schedule is and on the subjective risk perception by the taxpayers.

9.1 Measuring Marginal Tax Rates in the Survey

The conjecture that the German tax reform is responsible for the reduction in the extent of undeclared work cannot be substantiated by empirical data on individuals' actual tax payments. This information is not available. Another possibility would be to infer about the perceived tax burden. Asking about *perceived* marginal taxes instead of observing or asking about *actual* tax payments is not necessarily

DOI 10.1007/978-3-540-87401-0_9, © Springer-Verlag Berlin Heidelberg 2012

a second-best solution since actions are guided by perceptions of reality, and this has actually been done since 2004 (but not in the survey in 2001) by the following question:

> Suppose you were to earn an additional €100 per month (or earn €100 per month in total when otherwise unemployed). How much would you expect to keep after deduction of taxes and social security contributions?

Before turning to the results in Table 9.1, it should be noted that the question has been improved in the course of the survey period as explained in note (1) to the table: in the interviews carried out in August 2004, the respondents were asked to mention a tax rate between 0 and 100. As from October 2004, an extra question was added where respondents who did not know the exact tax rate were asked whether it was more than 75%, in the interval more than 50–75%, etc., and this raised the response rate by a few percentage points. In the interviews in 2006 and 2007, respondents were further asked if they had a Mini- or Midi-Job in mind when they answered the question. If the answer was yes, they were asked about their marginal tax in connection with a regular job.

Turning to the results, Table 9.1 shows that the average marginal tax rate decreased during the period, particularly from 2005 to 2006, which indicates – with the caveat mentioned below – that the respondents have incorporated the tax cuts in their perceptions. Had the control for Mini- and Midi-Jobs not been made in the surveys in 2006 and 2007, the marginal tax rates would only have been marginally lower – i.e. the vast majority of the respondents actually have had a regular job in mind in the first place when they answered the question. About 85% of the respondents answered the question and the average perceived marginal tax rate was about 45% in 2004–2005 decreasing to 41–42% in 2006–2007.

Table 9.1 Perceived marginal tax rate, 18–74-year-olds, Germany, 2004–2007, in percent

	Perceived marginal tax rate[a]				Total	No. of persons
	Average	In the interval [1;100]	Zero	Average		
2004	45.7	73.5	9.9	16.7	100	2,143
2005	44.8	76.3	10.4	13.4	100	2,144
2006	41.9	75.8	11.1	13.2	100	2,176
2007	41.1	72.9	12.0	15.1	100	1,096

Source: The Rockwool Foundation Research Unit's Shadow Economy Surveys

Note: The sample has been drawn at the household level, and a weight has been applied to make the sample representative as to gender and age distribution and other characteristics of the total population. The number of persons shown in the table is the actual number before the weight was applied

[a]The individual figures given ranged from 0% to 100%. In the interviews carried out in August 2004, the respondents were asked to mention a tax rate between 0 and 100. As from October 2004, an extra question was added where respondents who did not know the exact tax rate were asked whether it was more than 75%, in the interval more than 50–75%, etc., and this raised the response rate by a few percentage points. In the interviews in 2006 and 2007, respondents were further asked if they had a Mini- or Midi-Job in mind when they answered the question. If the answer was yes, they were asked about their marginal tax in connection with a regular job

The individual figures given ranged from 0% to 100%. Of the people who did respond, 10–12% had a zero marginal tax rate.

9.2 Marginal Tax by Geographical Regions

The results of differentiating the answers according to the respondents' address in either one of the new or one of the old Länder (states) are shown in Table 9.2.

Overall, the average marginal tax rate is either higher among respondents from West Germany than among respondents from East Germany or the rates are the same. The proportion with a zero marginal tax rate is lowest – and relatively constant – in the West, the exception being in 2005 where the rate among respondents from East Germany dropped to 6.3% compared with 11.4% among respondents from West Germany. While 11.4% is within the "normal" range of the answers given by respondents from West Germany in these four surveys – 9.0, 11.4, 8.9, and 12.2–6.3% is unusually low and outside the range of the answers given by respondents from East Germany – 13.3, 6.3, 19.4, and 12.2. The year after, a disproportionately *large* part – 19.4% – of the respondents from East Germany reported a zero marginal tax rate and in consequence the average marginal tax rate was unusually low, too, that year. The caveat mentioned in the previous section refers to this result: the average of 35.1% in East Germany is so low that it pulls the

Table 9.2 Perceived marginal tax rate, 18–74-year-olds, East and West Germany, 2004–2007, in percent

	Perceived marginal tax rate[a]				Total	No. of persons
	Average	In the interval [1;100]	Zero	Don't know/refusal		
2004 West	46.2	73.8	9.0	17.3	100	1,766
East	43.8	72.4	13.3	14.3	100	377
2005 West	44.7	75.4	11.4	13.2	100	1,677
East	44.9	79.7	6.3	14.1	100	467
2006 West	43.8	76.8	8.9	14.4	100	1,726
East	35.1	71.9	19.4	8.7	100	450
2007 West	41.4	72.2	12.0	15.9	100	859
East	40.1	75.8	12.2	12.0	100	237

Source: The Rockwool Foundation Research Unit's Shadow Economy Surveys

Note: The sample has been drawn at the household level, and a weight has been applied to make the sample representative as to gender and age distribution and other characteristics of the total population. The number of persons shown in the table is the actual number before the weight was applied.

[a]The individual figures given ranged from 0% to 100%. In the interviews carried out in August 2004, the respondents were asked to mention a tax rate between 0 and 100. In the interviews carried out in October 2004 and in April and June 2005, an extra question was added where respondents who did not know the exact tax rate were asked whether it was more than 75%, in the interval more than 50–75%, etc., and this raised the response rate by a few percentage points. In the interviews in 2006 and 2007, respondents were asked if they had a Mini- or Midi-Job in mind when they answered the question. If the answer was yes, they were asked about their marginal tax in connection with a regular job

overall average down. Again, the results of the interviews in 2006 stand out as they have done several times in the previous chapters. The low overall level in 2007 is supported by answers from both of the regions. Finally, the proportion of the respondents who refuses to answer or cannot answer the question about their marginal tax rate is lower in East Germany than in West Germany except from 2005 when it is slightly, but not significantly higher in the East.

9.3 An Econometric Analysis of Marginal Tax and Undeclared Work

Although the overall decline in undeclared work between 2001 and 2004 coincided with increases in deterrence, and although surveys carried out after 2004 suggest that the number of participants in the shadow economy may be back at the same level as in 2001, but the total amount of hours they spent on undeclared work has declined, this decline could be the result of other variables which have not been controlled for. For example, the tax and labor market reform acts in Germany could equally well have contributed to the reductions in the extent of undeclared work.

In this section we add the respondent's perceived marginal tax rate as explanatory variable in the regression analysis which we gradually expand from the starting point in Sect. 6.2 with only socio-economic variables. The perceived risk of being detected by the tax authorities if someone works without declaration and the expected punishment for this offence were added as explanatory (deterrence) variables in Sect. 8.3, and in Sect. 10.3, we close by adding variables to capture the possible impact of social norms on the propensity to carry out undeclared work.

The respondents' own perceived *marginal tax rate* is significant for women's probability of having carried out undeclared work. The indicator against this variable is in brackets, which means that the effect is only significant at the 10% level. However, it is closer to 5% than to 10%, but the effect disappears again when individual norms are included in the regressions in the next chapter. The effect stems from women in the group with lowest perceived marginal tax rates (0–19%) and being in this group increases the probability of having carried out undeclared work compared with the reference group (marginal tax rates in the interval 20–39% inclusive). Parallel to the regressions summarized in Table 9.3 and similar tables, we have performed regressions where we have added a dummy value which takes the value 1 if the respondent has not assessed his or her marginal tax and 0 otherwise. In the case of the marginal tax rate it makes a difference whether missing values are set to the median value of other answers or included as a dummy variable: missing marginal tax assessment is highly significant with a negative sign for male respondents. For female respondents it does not make any difference how missing values are treated.

Compared with the results summarized in Table 8.6 in Sect. 8.3, significant variables and significance levels remain the same. This means that being male

Table 9.3 Logistic regression of the probability of participating in undeclared work, 18–74-year-olds, Germany, 2004–2007

	Men	Women
Age	√	(√)
Marital status	–	√
Children under 6	–	–
Occupation	–	(√)
Education	(√)	–
Respondent's monthly net income	–	–
Length of unemployment	(√)	–
Region (East/West Germany)	(√)	–
Owner-occupied/not owner-occupied home	–	–
Year the survey was carried out	√	√
Perceived risk of detection	√	√
Perceived sanction if detected	–	–
Perceived marginal tax rate	*	(√)

Source: The Rockwool Foundation Research Unit's Shadow Economy Surveys
Note: √: significant effect at least at the 5% level, (√): significant effect but only at the 10% level, –: not significant. Details are shown in Appendix Table 10. *: if missing values are included via a dummy variable instead of being set to the median value, this variable becomes highly significant for men with a negative sign. The sample has been drawn at the household level, and a weight has been applied to make the sample representative as to gender and age distribution and other characteristics of the total population

under the age of 30 affects the probability of undeclared work positively – this effect is highly significant. Less significant is a positive effect from being female in the age group 30–39 years. However, this effect gains significance when marginal tax rates are included. Being in the age group 60–74 years has the opposite effect, but also at a low significance level. Significance is always relative to the reference group – in this case the 40–49-year-olds – and all other things being equal (ceteris paribus). A negative effect on the probability from being *married* remains very robust, but always only for women.

The effects of *occupation* and *education* are unchanged so a higher probability is found among unskilled women compared with the reference group (salaried workers) and among men with a Fachschule education compared with the education reference group (beruflich-betriebliche Ausbildung). The effect of Fachschule gains significance when missing values are included via a dummy variable instead of being set to the median value. *Length of unemployment* remains significant and positive for men and *region* still has the effect of reducing the probability – but only for men – if the address is in West Germany, but for both variables the significance decreases towards the limit which will remove them from the list of significant variables.

2006 is the only year where the *timing of the interviews* plays a significant role for men, but as stressed several times earlier this result is ambiguous. Among women, 2005 stands out as the only year and as a year with a particularly high level of participation in undeclared work compared with the reference year (2004), whereas the interviews carried out in 2006 or in 2007 still do not stand out as years with significantly higher or lower probabilities than the reference year.

If the perceived *risk of detection* is very high or fairly high it affects the probability strongly among women and relatively strongly among men – in both cases with a negative sign – when these respondents are compared with respondents who perceive the risk to be lower. Finally, the perceived *punishment* for working without declaration remains insignificant.

9.4 Summarizing the Main Findings

The overall decline in undeclared work between 2001 and 2004 coincided with increases in deterrence, and surveys carried out after 2004 suggest that although the number of participants in the shadow economy may be back at the same level as in 2001, the total amount of hours they spend on undeclared work has declined compared with 2001. Still, these observations could be the results of other things which have not been controlled for. For example, the tax and labor market reform acts in Germany could equally well have contributed to the reductions in the extent of undeclared work, and in this chapter we have dealt with the respondents' perceived marginal tax rate in order to try to capture the effect of tax policy.

It is a possibility that the German tax reform act of 2000, which has been implemented in stages up until 2005, could have affected the pattern of undeclared activities between 2001 and 2004 and later years, as the overall reduction in income taxes has been considerable in the recent past. Asking about *perceived* marginal taxes instead of observing or asking about *actual* tax payments is not necessarily a second-best solution in the efforts to investigate this question since actions are guided by perceptions of reality.

As was the case with the question about the expected punishment for carrying out undeclared work the question about marginal tax rates was also introduced in 2004 and it has been improved in the course of the survey period to minimize non-response and to make sure, that the respondents were not thinking of Mini-Jobs when they answered the question, which actually did not seem to be the case – the vast majority of the respondents actually have had a regular job in mind in the first place when they answered the question.

According to the answers, the average marginal tax rate decreased during the period from about 45% in 2004–2005 to 41–42% in 2006–2007. The fact that the decrease particularly took place from 2005 to 2006 indicates that the respondents have incorporated the tax cuts in their perceptions. Of the people who did respond, 10–12% had a zero marginal tax rate. Overall, the average marginal tax rate is either higher among respondents from West Germany than among respondents from East Germany or the rates are the same. Again, the results of the interviews in 2006 stand out as they have done several times in the previous chapters.

When the perceived marginal tax rate is added in the regression analysis which has been gradually expanded from the starting point with only socio-economic variables in Chap. 6, we find that the variable is significant at the 10% level for women's probability of having carried out undeclared work. However, we also revealed that the effect disappears again when individual norms are included in the regressions in the next chapter. The effect stems from women in the group with the lowest perceived marginal tax rates (0–19%) and being in this group increases the probability of having carried out undeclared work compared with the reference group (marginal tax rates in the interval 20–39% inclusive). An interesting result was that when missing values were treated via a dummy variable instead of being set to the median value, this variable actually becomes highly significant with a negative sign for men the interpretation of this being that if a person is insecure of what his marginal tax is, it has a negative impact on the probability of having participated in undeclared work. This effect remains when norms are added in the next chapter.

If the perceived risk of detection is very high or fairly high it affects the probability strongly among women and relatively strongly among men and in both cases with a negative sign. The perceived punishment for working without declaration remains insignificant.

Chapter 10
The Impact of Social Norms on Undeclared Work

In this chapter, we turn to the last of the main factors which, according to the economic theory of tax evasion, affect the extent of undeclared work. In the approach used by Allingham and Sandmo (1972), tax morale residually explains the level of tax compliance independent of tax policy and the behavior of state authorities. This argument is consistent with the view that fundamental social norms, such as religion or civic duty, shape tax morale. Feld and Frey (2007) provide a more elaborate discussion on which factors shape tax morale by establishing a relationship of social exchange. According to their approach, tax morale is endogenously driven by government behavior.

10.1 Measuring Social Norms in the Survey

In the present survey, a simple method of assessing social norms is implemented. Respondents received eight alternative examples of cheating behavior and for each had to assess on a scale from 1 to 10 whether they found this behavior absolutely unacceptable or absolutely acceptable or would place it somewhere in between. These assessments are summarized in Table 10.1. Such questions were not included until 2004.

Although respondents mostly found that the cheating behavior in question was absolutely unacceptable, there are interesting differences between the different types. If someone receives welfare benefits and other transfers without being entitled to get these payments, about three quarters of the respondents deem this behavior totally unacceptable. Taking a free ride on public transportation, i.e. buses and trains, is still absolutely unacceptable to half of the respondents. On the other hand, only one third of the respondents find carrying out undeclared work absolutely unacceptable.

There are additional interesting insights to get when a differentiation is made between undeclared work carried out by and for private individuals or households and undeclared work with firms involved. If a private household hires a private

L.P. Feld and C. Larsen, *Undeclared Work, Deterrence and Social Norms*,
DOI 10.1007/978-3-540-87401-0_10, © Springer-Verlag Berlin Heidelberg 2012

Table 10.1 Individual assessments of various kinds of cheating behavior, 18–74-year-olds, Germany, 2004–2007

	Average on a scale from 1 to 10[a]				Absolutely unacceptable[b]			
	2004	2005	2006	2007	2004 %	2005	2006	2007
Receiving welfare without entitlement	1.6	1.7	1.6	1.6	73.4	71.9	74.8	74.5
Free riding on bus/train	2.4	2.6	2.5	2.5	51.4	48.4	51.8	50.0
Undeclared work								
Carrying out	3.5	4.0	3.6	3.8	31.7	27.8	33.8	30.8
Private for private	4.4	5.0	4.6	4.6	24.7	20.3	26.5	23.9
Firm for private	2.7	3.1	2.9	3.0	47.9	41.8	45.9	43.8
Private for firm	1.9	2.1	2.0	2.1	62.8	62.0	63.8	59.7
Firm for firm	1.7	1.9	1.8	1.8	70.3	67.5	67.0	65.8
Tax evasion when declaring income	2.7	2.9	2.6	2.8	45.8	44.1	50.5	46.4

Source: The Rockwool Foundation Research Unit's Shadow Economy Surveys

Note: The sample has been drawn at the household level, and a weight has been applied to make the sample representative as to gender and age distribution and other characteristics of the total population

[a]Based on answers in the interval [1;10] where 1 is absolutely unacceptable and 10 is absolutely acceptable

[b]Respondents who refused to answer or who answered "Don't know" are included in these calculations. Depending on the question and the survey in question it was between 0% and 6% of the respondents who did not give an exact answer

person to do some work off the record and both parties to the transaction thus ignore the legal obligation to register and pay taxes and social security contributions, only one quarter of the respondents—and even fewer in the survey in 2005—assess this behavior as absolutely unacceptable.

As indicated, the acceptance of undeclared activities declines the more that firms are involved. If a private household hires a firm to do undeclared work, more than 40% of the respondents find this absolutely unacceptable. If a firm hires a private person for undeclared work, 60% or more evaluate this behavior as totally unacceptable and close to 70% find it absolutely unacceptable that a firm hires another firm to carry out undeclared work. Finally, if the question is about tax evasion in general, acceptance is lower than if the question is about carrying out undeclared work in general: 40–50% deem tax evasion absolutely unacceptable, which is about 15 percentage points more than in the case of carrying out undeclared work—and 20–25 percentage points lower than the evaluation of a situation where a private person works for a private household.

Calculating the average value of the answers is another way of getting an overview of how acceptable—or the opposite—various breaches of laws and regulations are. While a question about carrying out undeclared work in general, i.e. without specifying the parties involved, results in a degree of acceptance between 3.5 and 4.0, a more detailed specification of the supply side and the demand side in the transaction results in a 1 point higher degree of acceptance when both act in the capacity of private households.

The assessment of a firm carrying out undeclared work for a private household (between 2.7 and 3.1) was approximately the same as the assessment of tax evasion in general (between 2.6 and 2.9) and of the assessment of taking public transportation without buying a ticket (between 2.4 and 2.6) with activities mentioned in order of descending acceptance. When the question was about a private person working for a firm without declaration, or about two firms entering into such a transaction with each other on the supply and demand side respectively, the average acceptance decreased to about 2.0. Least accepted—average about 1.5—is receiving welfare payments without being entitled to. Overall, these assessments are quite consistent from one survey to the next.

10.2 Tax Morale by Geographical Regions

In this sub-section, we differentiate once again answers according to geographical region. It is apparent from Table 10.2 that receiving welfare payments without being entitled to is unacceptable to the majority of respondents in both regions. In three of the four surveys, a larger proportion of the respondents in West Germany deem it totally unacceptable than in East Germany. The assessments are also approximately at the same level when it comes to free riding on buses and trains and tax evasion in general but in these two cases it is the other way around as larger proportions of respondents in East than in West deem these types of behavior totally unacceptable. However, the *average* assessment is almost the same in the two parts of the country.

East Germans and West Germans also agree that undeclared work with firms involved is quite unacceptable in comparison with undeclared work carried out by and for private individuals or households. Undeclared work carried out by firms for private households is more accepted than when it is the other way around. In all three scenarios involving firms and undeclared work East Germans may be just slightly more approving than West Germans, but the real difference appears when the question is about undeclared work involving private individuals on both sides. This is significantly more accepted in East Germany than in West Germany, particularly in 2006 and 2007. All in all, this also leads to a slightly higher acceptance in East Germany than in West Germany of carrying out undeclared work in general. This is in accordance with the findings in previous chapters about the actual behavior in the shadow economy of the two groups. In East Germany, acceptance of undeclared work appears to have increased from 2004 to 2005–2007 in cases where private persons are involved on one or both sides of the transactions.

10.3 An Econometric Analysis of Social Norms and Undeclared Work

This section presents the last step in the empirical analysis where we first supplemented the socio-economic explanatory variables in Chap. 6 with deterrence variables in Chap. 8 and then added marginal tax rates in Chap. 9. Now we conduct

Table 10.2 Individual assessments of various types of cheating behavior, 18–74-year-olds, East and West Germany, 2004–2007

	Average on a scale from 1 to 10[a]				Absolutely unacceptable[b]			
	2004	2005	2006	2007	2004 %	2005	2006	2007
West Germany (Früheres Bundesgebiet)								
Receiving welfare without entitlement	1.5	1.6	1.6	1.5	74.6	72.8	75.4	74.0
Free riding on bus/train	2.4	2.6	2.5	2.6	49.7	46.3	51.5	46.6
Undeclared work								
Carrying out	3.4	3.8	3.7	3.7	31.8	27.5	34.3	32.5
Private for private	4.4	4.9	4.4	4.3	24.2	19.9	27.2	26.3
Firm for private	2.7	3.1	2.8	2.9	46.7	40.2	45.9	44.1
Private for firm	1.9	2.0	1.9	2.1	63.1	61.4	64.0	59.5
Firm for firm	1.6	1.8	1.8	1.8	70.4	68.5	66.1	65.3
Tax evasion when declaring income	2.7	2.9	2.6	2.8	44.3	41.5	48.7	44.5
East Germany (Neue Länder)								
Receiving welfare without entitlement	1.7	2.1	1.7	1.6	68.8	68.2	72.6	76.1
Free riding on bus/train	2.4	2.6	2.8	2.1	57.8	56.6	52.9	63.2
Undeclared work								
Carrying out	3.7	4.4	4.2	4.3	31.4	29.0	32.1	24.3
Private for private	4.7	5.4	5.4	5.5	26.7	22.1	23.6	14.8
Firm for private	2.7	3.2	3.3	3.2	52.7	48.2	46.0	42.7
Private for firm	2.0	2.3	2.1	2.2	61.4	64.3	63.3	60.6
Firm for firm	1.8	2.1	1.9	1.9	69.9	63.1	70.1	67.8
Tax evasion when declaring income	2.6	2.7	2.5	2.6	51.9	54.4	57.4	53.8

Source: The Rockwool Foundation Research Unit's Shadow Economy Surveys
Note: The sample has been drawn at the household level, and a weight has been applied to make the sample representative as to gender and age distribution and other characteristics of the total population
[a]Based on answers in the interval [1;10] where 1 is absolutely unacceptable and 10 is absolutely acceptable
[b]Respondents who refused to answer or who answered "Don't know" are included in these calculations. Depending of the question and the survey in question it was between 0% and 6% of the respondents who did not give an exact answer

logistic regressions in which we include the indicators of social norms in addition to the variables that have been considered so far to see which impact they have on the probability of participating in undeclared work.

As the category to be left out, we chose free riding on public transportation because it has least to do with undeclared work of the examples of cheating behavior we have asked about in the surveys. The expected signs of the variables considered cannot be easily inferred, however, due to the fact that their impact must be assessed relative to free riding on public transportation. The way this is done in practice is that the answer to each of the other norm questions is divided by the answer to the question about free riding on public transportation.

Table 10.3 and Appendix Tables 11, 12 and 13 report the results. First, *social norms* have a significant impact on the probability of carrying out undeclared work,

Table 10.3 Logistic regression of the probability of participating in undeclared work, 18–74-year-olds, Germany, 2004–2007

	Missing: set to median[a]			Missing as dummy[b]		
	Men	Women	Men and women	Men	Women	Men and women
Gender			√			√
Age	√	√	√	√	√	√
Marital status	–	√	√	–	√	√
Children under 6	–	–	–	–	–	–
Occupation	–	(√)	(√)	–	√	√
Education	√	–	√	√	–	√
Respondent's monthly net income	–	–	–	(√)	–	–
Length of unemployment	√	–	(√)	√	–	–
Region (East/West Germany)	*	*	(√)	*	*	(√)
Owner-occupied/not owner-occupied home	–	–	(√)	(√)	–	(√)
Year the survey was carried out	√	√	√	√	√	√
Perceived risk of detection[a, b]	*	√	√	*	√	√
Perceived sanction if detected[a, b]	–	–	–	–	–	–
Perceived marginal tax rate[a, b]	–	–	–	√	–	(√)
Social norms[a, b]	√	√	√	√	√	√

Source: The Rockwool Foundation Research Unit's Shadow Economy Surveys

Note: √: significant effect at least at the 5% level, (√): significant effect but only at the 10% level, –: not significant. Details are shown in Appendix Tables 11–13. *: if data collected in 2008, which could not be analyzed in time to be fully integrated in the manuscript for the present publication, is included in the regression, the variable becomes significant. The sample has been drawn at the household level, and a weight has been applied to make the sample representative as to gender and age distribution and other characteristics of the total population. [a,b] Missing values in the qualitative variables (risk, sanction, marginal tax and social norms) are included in two different ways

[a]First, missing values in the qualitative variables are set to the median value of the answers from the respondents who expressed a concrete assessment

[b]Second, missing values are then included via dummy variables which take the value 1 if the respondent has not answered the question by expressing a concrete assessment and 0 otherwise

but it is not the same variables that are significant in the respective regressions for men and women. For women, it is those with a relatively high degree of acceptance of arrangements where private individuals carry out undeclared work for other private individuals or households who have a significantly higher probability of having carried out undeclared work themselves compared with other respondents. For men, the significant variable is a relatively high degree of acceptance of arrangements where firms carry out undeclared work for private individuals or households. As mentioned, this is measured relative to free riding on public transportation. However, if we include 2008, this changes to private to private undeclared work arrangements for men as well, but at a lower significance level.

For men, acceptance of social security fraud also is significant, but with a negative sign. Joint regressions for men and women point to social security fraud (negative impact) and private to private undeclared work arrangements (positive impact) and—especially in the regressions based on data from 2004 to 2007, but to a lesser degree when 2008 is added—also firm to private undeclared work arrangements (positive impact).

Second, *deterrence* does not have any significant effect on male undeclared work activity in the regression based on pooled data from the period 2004 to 2007 when norms are included. On the other hand, as illustrated by the asterisk in Table 10.3, this is the only example where *risk* loses its significance. When the data for 2008, which will be published in more detail in a forthcoming study, is added, risk becomes significant for men again, and also in the joint regressions for men and women, risk is a highly significant variable with a negative sign like it is in the separate regressions for women. Overall, the conclusion as far as *deterrence* is concerned is that perceived *risk* of detection must be considered an important variable, even though it becomes insignificant in one regression for men. This, however, is the only example, where risk is not significant at least at the 5% level.

The perceived level of *punishment* does not reach significance at least at the 10% level in regressions based on pooled data sets, although the sanction variables actually are significant (to a varying degree) and have the expected signs in 2005 as well as in 2007 in regressions for men.

Third, the perceived *marginal tax rate* is significant for men who do not assess the exact rate while no significant differences are found between a low perceived marginal tax rate and medium or high rates when social norms are included.

Fourth, as to *socio-economic variables*, significant effects are found from gender, marital status, occupation, education, income, length of unemployment, home-ownership, region and year of the interview.

Being *male* has a positive sign, like being in the age group *18–29 years* old has for men and being in the age group *30–39 years* has for women, while being in the age group *60–74 years* has the opposite effect, but especially for men. The latter effect is most significant for men and, in the joint regressions for men and women, in the one based on interviews from 2004 to 2007.

Being *married* has a negative sign for women in the separate regressions but the variable is also highly significant in the joint regressions for men and women. Being an *unskilled* woman has a positive, but not highly significant, impact on the probability as long as 2008 is not included, and in the joint regressions for men and women the occupational groups *skilled and unskilled* both affect probability, but not in a highly significant way either, and these variables become insignificant when 2008 is included.

Having a *Fachschule* education has a positive sign but, on the other hand, the variable loses significance when the data from 2008 is included and in the joint regressions for men and women based on data from 2004 to 2008, the variable does not become significant until all variables are included. *Hochschule* becomes significant at the 10% level with a positive sign for women in the pooled regressions based on 2004–2007.

A monthly own net income in the range *€500–999* is significant and positive at the 10% level for men in the pooled regression based on 2004–2007, but otherwise not. In case of unemployment, the *length of the unemployment period* is significant with a positive sign for men in the pooled regressions based on 2004–2007 and, but at the lowest significance level of 10%, in the joint regressions for men and women based on the same period, but when 2008 data is added it becomes insignificant.

Being an *owner-occupier* is significant at the 10% level in the joint regressions for men and women and in the regressions for men where missing values are included via dummy variables. Living in the *Western part of Germany* has a negative sign, and this geographical variable gains significantly in importance when data from 2008 is included. In the pooled regressions conducted separately for men and women based on interviews from the years 2004–2007, this variable is only significant for men. The year the interview was carried out is significant in every regression, but if *2006* is ignored it cannot be ruled out that the participation rate was the same for men every year, while *2005* stand out as highly significant and with a positive sign for women.

The overall performance of the model increases somewhat as measured by the Log pseudolikelihood statistics and also by the Pseudo R^2 not reported in the appendix tables.

10.4 Summarizing the Main Findings

If someone receives welfare benefits and other transfers without being entitled to get these payments, about three quarters of the respondents deem this behavior totally unacceptable and taking a free ride on public transportation is absolutely unacceptable to half of the respondents. On the other hand, if a private household hires a private person to work off the record, only one quarter of the respondents assess this behavior as absolutely unacceptable. The acceptance of undeclared activities declines the more that firms are involved. Finally, if the question is about tax evasion in general, acceptance is lower than if the question is about carrying out undeclared work in general. Overall, these assessments are quite consistent from one survey to the next.

The real difference between the Eastern and Western parts of Germany appears when the question is about undeclared work involving private individuals on both sides. This is significantly more accepted in East Germany than in West Germany, particularly in 2006 and 2007. All in all, this also leads to a slightly higher acceptance in East Germany than in West Germany of carrying out undeclared work in general. This is in accordance with the findings in previous chapters about the actual behavior in the shadow economy of the two groups. In East Germany, acceptance of undeclared work appears to have increased from 2004 to 2005–2007 in cases where private persons are involved on one or both sides of the transactions.

When social norms are included in the logistic regression analyses, it is still very significant that being male and being young increases the probability of having carried out undeclared work. In the separate regressions, 18–29-year-old men and 30–39-year-old women have a significantly higher probability of having carried out undeclared work than the reference group (40–49-year-old men and women respectively), and the 60–74-year-olds have a lower probability. Both effects are strongest in the regressions for men, and in a joint regression for men and women, the age group 30–39 years does not differ significantly from the reference group.

For women, and in a joint regression for men and women, being married has a strong and negative effect. The most persistent effect of education is that having completed Fachschule increases the probability of conducting undeclared work and being either a skilled or an unskilled worker has the same effect, but these effects are not particularly strong in these regressions and the latter is only found in the separate regressions for women, and—like being a skilled worker—in a joint regression for men and women based on 2004–2007.

A certain, but not particularly high significance level is found for those having a monthly own net income in the range €500–999, for the length of an unemployment period and from being an owner-occupier, in all instances with a positive sign, and in all instances only for men. Living in the Western part of Germany has a negative sign, but this effect is not significant in separate regressions for men and women based on pooled data from 2004 to 2007, only in a joint regression for men and women. However, this geographical variable gains significantly in importance when the data from 2008, which we have referred to occasionally, are included. The year of the interview is significant in every regression, but if the ambiguous results from 2006 are ignored, it cannot be ruled out that the participation rate was the same for men every year, while 2005 stands out as highly significant and with a positive sign for women.

The perceived marginal tax rate is significant with a negative sign for men who did not assess the exact rate—an effect which remains in the joint regression for men and women, but at a lower significance level—while no significant differences are found between a low perceived marginal tax rate and medium or high rates when social norms are included. The relatively weak effect in terms of significance level we found for women in the group with the lowest marginal tax rates before social norms were considered disappears with norms included.

The differentiated results from Table 10.3 reveal an interesting pattern of how social norms affect undeclared work. For men, a higher acceptance of receiving welfare without entitlement is associated with a *lower* probability of carrying out undeclared work. Women who more readily accept the type of undeclared work characterized by a private to private arrangement have a *higher* probability of carrying out undeclared work themselves while for men the significant variable includes firm to private arrangements. These results rather indicate a positive relationship between social norms and undeclared work: *the less accepted different kinds of undeclared activities are, the less probable it is that a person has carried out undeclared work.* Only cheating on transfer payments leads to the opposite effect: the more accepted cheating on transfer payments is, the less probable it is that a person has carried out undeclared work. It may then perhaps be easier to cheat on the transfer system than to do undeclared work.

In addition, social norms and deterrence measures in the form of the risk of being detected conducting undeclared work appear to be equally important and social norms appear to be more important than the expected punishment if detected. Even though deterrence turned out not to have any significant effect on male undeclared work activity in a regression based on pooled data from the period 2004–2007 when norms are included, this was the only example were risk is not significant at least at the 5% level. When the data for 2008, which will be published in more detail in a forthcoming study, is added, risk becomes significant for men again, and also in joint regressions for men and women based on 2004–07, risk is a highly significant variable with a negative sign like it is in the separate regressions for women. Overall, the conclusion as far as deterrence is concerned is that perceived risk of detection must be considered an important variable together with social norms, even though the risk variable becomes insignificant in one regression for men.

Chapter 11
Conclusions

In recent years, the German government has undertaken several steps to increase tax compliance and to fight undeclared work—also known as "Schwarzarbeit"—by raising the level of deterrence. This has mainly been done by increasing audit rates, but also by higher fines. While these policies have been particularly aimed at fighting undeclared work, agreements at the international level as well as a relaxation of the German bank secrecy laws also target the individual propensity to evade capital income taxes, and it is the stated goal of the German Federal Finance Ministry to fight tax evasion at all levels, from the international capital markets to housekeeping services.

Theoretically, deterrence—defined as the product of the probability of detection and fines—often appears to be *the* policy instrument of choice to reduce undeclared work in addition to tax policy. However, it can be expected that, similar to other kinds of tax evasion, undeclared work will be heavily influenced by tax morale, which is shaped by maintaining a long-term relationship between the state and the citizens. Citizens and the state are engaged in an implicit psychological tax contract that binds both contractual partners in a social exchange relationship, according to which citizens pay their fair share for the public services they receive. As with any private contract, the psychological tax contract must be backed by the law, so that deterrence plays a role. However, it is equally important to provide the public services that citizens want in exchange for tax payments and to treat taxpayers as contractual partners instead of inferiors in a hierarchical relationship. Excessive deterrence may thus backfire on such a psychological tax contract, because it could crowd out tax morale and thereby lead to more undeclared work and more tax evasion (Feld and Frey 2007). Higher deterrence levels will thus not necessarily reduce the incidence or extent of undeclared work.

In this study, the relationship between deterrence and undeclared work in Germany is analyzed by including both the perceived risk of detection and the perceived sanction if detected. The analyses are based on, as yet, seven series of interviews carried out from August 2004 to March 2007. Future analyses will benefit from the inclusion of additional data from two series of interviews in 2008 which could not be analyzed in time to be fully integrated in the present

L.P. Feld and C. Larsen, *Undeclared Work, Deterrence and Social Norms*,

DOI 10.1007/978-3-540-87401-0_11,

publication. The results of the 2008 survey will be published in a study in German but we have chosen to refer to some of its main results already now when they bring additional insights of significance to the overall conclusions. Results up to and including 2006 have been published in Feld and Larsen (2005, 2006 and 2008).

In addition, developments in the area of undeclared work are documented in relation to the findings of the 2001 study conducted by Pedersen (2003). Following his approach, a survey design is chosen for the empirical analysis because it is the only approach based on field data that allows the testing of the impact of deterrence on undeclared work, given the current state of research in this field in Germany. German tax secrecy laws prohibit the use of data comparable to that used in the U.S. Taxpayer Compliance Measurement Program. Aggregate data, at the German state level for example, do not help, because state fiscal authorities do not provide information on the size of fines and the level of control intensities. In the survey approach, it is possible however to ask respondents about their perception of the risk of being detected and of the size of fines, in addition to asking about their participation in undeclared work. Measuring deterrence (and norms, etc.) is thus the most important advantage of the survey method as compared to other methods used to measure the incidence and extent of undeclared activities. In addition, the survey method allows the analysis of undeclared work in detail, as the various elements comprising the shadow economy (undeclared work at less than full price (the topic of this study), non-declaration of earned income and sales at full market price, illegal economic activities, non-declaration of capital or transfer income, etc.) can be differentiated. Furthermore, undeclared work can be measured in terms of payment in cash, but also in terms of payment in kind, or in the form of a quid pro quo.

As emphasized several times in this study, the survey approach, like any other method, has its drawbacks, as respondents may not tell the truth or the whole truth, and there is always a certain amount of non-response which can give a distorted picture of the true extent of the phenomenon. This shortcoming can be overcome partly by a structured interview in which the interviewer pays particular attention to the slightest indication that respondents are understating the true extent of their participation in undeclared work. This can be done by repeating the relevant questions, or by underlining that the survey is exclusively used for scientific purposes and does not involve any personal disadvantage for the respondent. The strategy of using a structured interview technique has indeed been followed in this study but, still, the data produced by the survey method represent the lower limit of the estimated extent of undeclared work in Germany.

Response rates and refusals were almost unchanged from survey to survey from 2001 to 2004–2007 at levels of 64–66% and 16–17% respectively. The analysis is primarily based on the 18–74-year-olds, and 2,143 observations were used in the empirical analysis of undeclared work in 2004, 2,144 in 2005, 2,176 in 2006, and 1,096 in 2007, while the sample in 2001 consisted of 5,686 persons aged 18–74. According to the survey results, the proportion of the total population in the group 18–74 years who stated that they had carried out undeclared work themselves within the last 12 months decreased from 10.4% in 2001 to 8.8% in 2004, but only to increase to 11.1% in 2005. Then the participation rate dropped dramatically to 5.8% but, as it has been emphasized several times throughout this study, this and other results from the 2006 survey must be interpreted with care, as it is obvious that particularly one and possibly both of the two series of interviews that year have been biased in some way. This is supported by the fact that the participation rate was back at 9.7% in 2007 (and 9.6% in 2008).

The participation rate in undeclared work among men has been relatively stable at 13–16%, highest in 2007, if we ignore the ambiguous year 2006 (7.8%), while that among women first decreased from 6.5% to 4.5%, then increased to 8.5 in 2005 and decreased again to 3.9% in 2006 and 3.8% in 2007. Looking more closely at the age structure of the participants in undeclared work at the beginning of the period, the highest participation rates are found in the youngest age groups, but the 18–29-year-olds appear to have reduced their participation to a level close to that of the 30–39-year-olds who are characterized by a remarkably stable participation rate of about 12–13%. A remarkable stability is also characteristic of the 40–49-year-olds at a somewhat lower level of about 9–11% as participation is decreasing by age. Generally, the occupational groups with the highest representation on the undeclared labor market have been self-employed/assisting spouses, skilled workers, unemployed persons and students. A very pronounced reduction in undeclared work among the self-employed and assisting spouses from 2001 to 2004 is unlikely to reflect solely a change in participation in undeclared work, despite the fact that the increase in deterrence in 2004 was aimed mainly at this group. It rather underlines the possibility that respondents' readiness to answer questions about undeclared work may have changed, too, at least temporarily. Self-employed/assisting spouses actually increased their participation every year since 2004—even in 2006 where all other rates dropped dramatically.

The average time spent per week on undeclared work has gradually been reduced from 8¼ h per week in 2001 to 6¼ h in 2007. Men who carry out undeclared work spend more time on such activities than women engaged in such activities do, and the relative difference has become larger, as men reduced their undeclared working week from 8½ h to 6½ h, while women reduced their undeclared working week from just under 8 h to just under 5½ h. Except for the 30–39-year-olds who increased average time spent to almost 9 h per week, all other age groups reduced their average number of undeclared working hours per week during the period. In 2007, the 30–39-year-olds thus is the age group with the highest participation rate, together with the 20–29-year-olds, and the longest working week in the undeclared sector of the economy. It must be kept in mind, however, that the survey in 2007 is based on only one wave consisting of about 1,100 interviews.

The hourly compensation for undeclared work remained virtually unchanged between 2001 and 2004 with an increase by 10 cents from 10.30€ to 10.40€ in that time period, but then increased to 12–13 Euros in 2005–2007. At the beginning of the period, men had an hourly wage of about 11 Euros, while women earned about 8½ Euro an hour. Whereas men benefited most from a wage increase from 2004 to 2005, so the gender differential also increased, this development was reversed the following years.

Overall, there was a 24% decrease in the extent of undeclared work in Germany, from 4.1% relative to official GDP in 2001 to 3.1% in 2004, measured on the basis of the wages pertaining in the official economy approximated by undeclared hours as a percentage of declared working hours. Even though the participation rate increased to its highest level measured in these surveys in 2005, the total amount of undeclared work did not reach the level found in 2001, because the average number of hours spent on such activities continued to decrease. From 3.6% in 2005, undeclared work dropped to 1.8% in 2006. In 2006, the participation rate was unusually low while the average number of hours spent per week on, and the average hourly payment for, undeclared work did not differ from the general picture. In 2007 (and 2008), the participation was back at its apparently "normal" level of around 10%, but the average number of hours decreased further resulting in an estimate of 3.2% relative to official GDP in 2007 (and 2.3% in 2008).

Calculating the size of the undeclared sector using the actual hourly wages paid, which, by definition, are lower than the market price because taxes due etc. are not paid, there was a 25% decrease from a little more than 1.3 "percent of GDP" in 2001 to 1.0% in 2004. The highest level was found in 2005 at 1.4%, while the extremely low participation rate caused it to drop to 0.6% in 2006. In 2007, the rate was 1.0% (0.8% in 2008). If all these undeclared hours had been converted to working hours in the formal economy, it would have corresponded to 1.63 million full-time jobs in 2001. If the same distribution of alternatives to using undeclared labor applied to Germany as to Denmark, meaning that perhaps one third could be converted to work at the formal labor market, that would still amount to almost 550,000 jobs at market prices including taxes, VAT and social security contributions in 2001; in 2004: 420,000; 2005: 470,000; 2006: 240,000; and 2007: 380,000.

The proportion of respondents who either had carried out undeclared work or would be willing to do so if given the chance decreased slightly from 25.5% in 2001 to 24.4% in 2004, while the proportion who neither had done nor would undertake such work increased from 54.2% to 61.9%. In 2005, this "potential" work force consisting of those who either had carried out undeclared work or who would consider the possibility of doing so amounted to 28.6% while 56.3 had not and would also decline an offer to do so. In 2006 and 2007, these proportions were 20.3/67.7% and 26.0/59.9% respectively, which again more than indicate that the answers that were obtained in 2006 were biased one way or the other.

A closer look at how undeclared work is distributed across sectors of the economy as an average for the whole period places about one third of the hours worked without declaration in "construction" while "public and personal services" and "the primary sector" (agriculture etc. including gardening) both account for about 10%. "Financial intermediation and business activities", "transport and telecommunications", "sales and repairs", and "hotels and restaurants" all, on average, lie in the range 5% to less than 10%, while "manufacturing" shows a very constant level around 1%.

The distribution of undeclared activities may also be illustrated by looking at the number of hours worked without declaration as a proportion of the number of working hours in the formal part of the economy in each sector. Such calculations also found the largest proportion in the construction sector. Over the period as a whole, including the ambiguous results in 2006, about one in every 10 h worked in construction was undeclared. We estimated that while the total number of hours worked in the formal part of the construction sector had decreased by about 20% in 2004–2005 compared with 2001, the undeclared part of construction work measured in hours increased by 15%, thus reducing the overall decline in (declared + undeclared) working hours in construction to 15–16%.

It is difficult to spot a clear picture for the second most important group, the primary sector, which includes gardening as an important component, because of some large fluctuations, but undeclared hours' share of the total number of hours worked appears to have been declining slightly. Undeclared hours' share of the total number of hours worked in the hotels and restaurants sector is, on average, about 5% as in the transport and telecommunications sector. In other sectors, proportions are lower. In manufacturing, the proportion is negligible.

Geographically, the amounts of undeclared work carried out by people living in the Western and Eastern parts of Germany respectively measured relative to their formal labor market participation were quite close in 2001, but a marked divergence has occurred since then. Again we use undeclared hours as a proportion of declared working hours as a proxy for undeclared work as "percent of GDP" at formal market prices—or rather relative to GDP, as some undeclared work is already included in official GDP. This estimate remained between 4% and 5% in East, the only exception being 2006, while the overall decreasing trend for the country as a whole is due to the development in Western Germany from just over 4% in 2001 to an average of approximately 3% when 2006 is disregarded.

Undeclared work thus seems to have kept its importance in the Eastern parts of Germany, whereas its importance appears to have decreased in West, which is interesting both in the light of the continuous campaigns against undeclared work (and other kinds of tax evasion) and given the results presented in *Chapter 3* which indicate higher tax morale in the East as compared to the West.

Though overall this may look like a success for the deterrence policies of recent years, the descriptive evidence is not sufficient to establish this impact, because other factors could equally well have led to a reduction in undeclared work. The recent German tax reforms with reductions in income taxes and/or labor market reforms could have induced the same outcome.

Our study establishes first that the recent deterrence policy is reflected in individual perceptions, as the individually perceived risk of being detected and punished for carrying out undeclared work increased between 2001 and 2004 from 36% to about 39% and to more than 40% in 2005–2007.

Questions about how severe the respondents would expect the sanctions to be were not included until 2004, and the questions were adjusted during the period, which may complicate the interpretation of this variable somewhat. With this in mind, the overall conclusion was that respondents' perceptions do not indicate an increase in the size of sanctions for carrying out undeclared work and the accompanying tax evasion etc. A differentiation according to region does not reveal any systematic differences between East and West Germany except that there seems to be a tendency for respondents from East Germany to expect imprisonment more often than respondents from West Germany do.

In the subsequent multivariate analyses (logistic regressions) of the probability of participating in undeclared work, it turned out that of the two deterrence variables, it is only the risk of detection as such that appears to have an impact when other factors such as socio-demographic characteristics and income are kept constant. Other things like age and marital status appeared to be much more important determinants than the perceived sanction. It should be noted that we are looking for correlations between explanatory variables and participation (1) as opposed to not participating (0) in undeclared work, and that if we find such correlations it is not the same as to say that we have found causal relationships.

A rather preliminary econometric analysis based solely on socio-economic explanatory variables and the year of the survey found that the probability of having carried out undeclared work is higher for young men (18–29 years old) and lower for the 60–74-year-olds; single women are more likely to carry out undeclared work than married women; being a skilled worker irrespective of gender, an unskilled woman or a female student also correlated with undeclared work. Men who have completed Fachschule also have a significantly higher probability of having carried out undeclared work than the reference group; low income increases the probability to conduct undeclared work, too. In case of unemployment, the length of the period without a job increases the probability, but only for men. Finally, women's participation is significantly lower at the end of the period than at the beginning while the hypothesis cannot be rejected that the participation rate for men has been constant throughout the period.

When the first of the deterrence variables—risk of detection—is entered into a regression analysis to see how it correlates with participation in undeclared work, we find that if the risk of detection is perceived to be very high or fairly high it has a negative effect on the probability of having carried out undeclared work, and this effect is highly significant for women as well as for men. The inclusion of risk does not change what has just been written about socio-economic variables.

When sanctions are included in order to capture the full effect of deterrence, data from 2001 has to be omitted, because such questions were not asked until 2004. One consequence of this is a decrease in the number of significant effects and in the level of significance compared with the regressions with 2001 included, e.g., the effect of risk loses significance for men. This is an effect of omitting data from 2001, not an effect of including sanctions. Omitting data from 2001 also makes region significant for men—although it is only at a low significance level—so those who live in West Germany have a lower probability of answering yes than those who live in East Germany. These regressions simultaneously account for age, marital status, children, occupation, education, income, unemployment period, region, home ownership, year and deterrence. The regressions have been conducted separately for men and women.

The perceived risk of detection appears to have a strong effect among women and a relatively strong effect among men; in both cases with the expected (negative) sign, when respondents who perceive the risk to be high are compared with respondents who perceive the risk to be low. The effects of the variables which measure the perceived level of sanctions for evasion of tax and social security payments connected with undeclared work do not reach any conventional significance level, although they have the expected signs, too. Overall, this evidence at least partly appears to be in favor of the hypothesis that deterrence is the policy of choice for a fight against undeclared work.

However, this is before taxes and social norms are included as explanatory variables. Given the efforts of the German Federal government to reduce the tax burden on labor and capital as well as to increase the incentives to start work in the official labor market for transfer recipients, it is interesting to investigate the extent to which the recent reductions in tax rates could have had an effect on the probability of carrying out undeclared work. An investigation of the possible effects of labor market reforms is beyond the scope of this study.

According to the answers in the surveys, the average marginal tax rate decreased during the period from about 45% in 2004–2005 to 41–42% in 2006–2007. The fact that the decrease particularly took place from 2001 to 2005 indicates that the respondents have incorporated the tax cuts in their perceptions. As far as region is concerned, the average marginal tax rate is either higher in the Western parts of Germany than in the Eastern parts of the country, or the rates are the same. Also in this respect, the results of the interviews in 2006 stand out with a different distribution of the answers than in other years as they have done several times in other questions.

When the perceived marginal tax rate is added in the regression analyses together with the explanatory variables mentioned above—socio-economic variables, risk and sanctions—we find that it increases the probability for women if they belong to the group with the lowest perceived marginal tax rates (0–19%). However, this variable is only significant at the 10% level and the effect disappears again when individual norms are included in the regressions. As a starting point, the non-negligible number of missing values in the qualitative variables (risk of detection, sanctions, marginal tax and social norms) have been set to the median value of the answers from respondents who expressed their assessments, but an interesting result is that when missing values are included via a dummy variable instead, this dummy variable actually becomes highly significant for men and with a negative sign. The interpretation of this is that if a person is insecure of what his marginal tax is, it has a negative impact on his probability of having participated in undeclared work. As opposed to the effect of a low marginal tax found in the regression for women, this effect remains significant when norms are added, but it is never significant for women.

Compared with the results of the previous regressions, other variables keep their significance levels. Being male under the age of 30 affects the probability of undeclared work positively and this effect is highly significant. Less significant is a positive effect from being female in the age group 30–39 years. This effect became significant when sanctions were added and gains further significance when social norms are included. Being in the age group 60–74 years has the opposite effect, but the effect is more significant for men than for women.

A negative effect on the probability from being married remains very robust in the separate regressions for women and in the joint regressions for men and women.

A higher probability is found among unskilled women compared with the reference group (salaried workers) and among men with a Fachschule education compared with the education reference group (beruflich-betriebliche Ausbildung). Two effects which are also only significant for men are the length of an unemployment period which increases probability, and region which has the effect of reducing the probability if the address is in West Germany, but for both variables significance decreases towards the limit which will remove them from the list of significant variables.

Ignoring the ambiguous result from the survey in 2006, the only year which really stands out is 2005 in the regression for women as a year with a particularly high level of participation in undeclared work compared with the reference year (2004). The interviews carried out in 2006 and in 2007 still do not stand out as years with significantly higher or lower probabilities than 2004.

If the perceived risk of detection is very high or fairly high it affects the probability strongly among women and relatively strongly among men and in both cases with a negative sign. The perceived punishment for working without declaration remains insignificant.

Finally, the impact of social norms on undeclared work was analyzed. When they were asked to distinguish between different kinds of cheating behavior, three quarters of the respondents evaluated benefit cheating, e.g., that someone receives welfare benefits or other transfers without being entitled to get these payments, as totally unacceptable. Taking a free ride on public transportation was absolutely unacceptable to half of the respondents. However, only one quarter of the respondents deemed it absolutely unacceptable that a private household hires a private person to do some work off the record. In differentiating the different kinds of undeclared work, respondents indicated that the more firms are involved, the less acceptable is the transaction. Overall, these assessments are quite consistent from one survey to the next. The multivariate analyses summarized below corroborate these findings: social norms have a highly significant impact on the probability of having carried out undeclared work according to the answers in the surveys underlying this study.

The real difference between the Eastern and Western parts of Germany in this respect appears to be that undeclared work involving private individuals on both sides is significantly more accepted in East Germany than in West Germany, particularly in 2006 and 2007. All in all, this also leads to a slightly higher acceptance in East Germany than in West Germany of carrying out undeclared work in general. This is in accordance with the findings in previous chapters about the actual behavior in the shadow economy of the two groups. In East Germany, acceptance of undeclared work appears to have increased from 2004 to 2005–2007 in cases where private persons are involved on one or both sides of the transactions.

With social norms included in the logistic regression analyses, it is still very significant that being male and young increases the probability of having carried out undeclared work. For women the relevant age group is the 30–39-year-olds.

60–74-year-olds have a lower probability. In separate regressions, the effects of age are strongest in the regressions for men, and in the joint regressions for men and women, the age group 30–39 years does not differ significantly from the reference group (40–49 years). For women, and in a joint regression for men and women, being married has a strong and negative effect. The most persistent effect of education is that having completed Fachschule increases the probability of conducting undeclared work and being either a skilled or an unskilled worker has the same effect, but it is not particularly strong effects according to the regression results presented here and the latter is only found in the separate regressions for women, and in a joint regression for men and women based on 2004–2007.

A monthly own net income in the range of 500–999€, the length of an unemployment period and being an owner-occupier all have a certain, but not particularly high significance level in the regression for men, and in all instances the coefficient has a positive sign. Living in the Western part of Germany has a negative sign, but this effect is not significant in separate regressions for men and women based on pooled data from 2004 to 2007, only in a joint regression for men and women. However, this geographical variable gains significantly in importance when the data from 2008, which we have referred to occasionally, are included.

If the ambiguous results from 2006 are ignored, it cannot be ruled out that the participation rate was the same for men every year, while 2005 stand out as highly significant and with a positive sign for women.

As far as the possible effect of tax policy is concerned—represented by the effect of respondents' individually perceived marginal tax rates on the probability of having carried out undeclared work—these regressions did not lead to any significant differences between a low perceived marginal tax rate and medium or high rates when social norms are included. A relatively weak and negative effect found for women in the group with the lowest marginal tax rates before social norms were considered disappears with norms included. The only significant effect left with norms included is found for men who did not assess the exact marginal tax rate, but it may be difficult to see the policy implications of this—negative—effect.

Social norms affect the probability of having carried out undeclared work in these surveys. For men, a higher acceptance of receiving welfare without entitlement is associated with a lower probability of carrying out undeclared work, whereas a higher acceptance of private households hiring firms to work off the record has the opposite effect. Women who more readily accept the type of undeclared work characterized by a private to private arrangement also have a higher probability of carrying out undeclared work themselves. These results rather indicate a positive relationship between social norms and undeclared work: the less accepted different kinds of undeclared activities are, the less probable it is that a person has carried out undeclared work. Only cheating on transfer payments leads to the opposite effect: the more accepted cheating on transfer payments is, the less probable it is that a person has carried out undeclared work. It would then be easier to cheat on the transfer system than to do undeclared work.

All in all, social norms and deterrence measures in the form of the risk of being detected by the authorities when conducting undeclared work appear to be equally important and social norms and the risk of detection appear to be more important than the expected punishment if detected. Even though deterrence turned out not to have any significant effect on male undeclared work activity in a regression based on pooled data from the period 2004 to 2007 when norms are included, this was the only example were risk is not significant at least at the 5% level. When the data for 2008, which will be published in more detail in a forthcoming study, is added, risk is highly significant for men again, and also in joint regressions for men and women based on 2004–07, risk is a highly significant variable with a negative sign like it is in the separate regressions for women. Overall, the conclusion as far as deterrence is concerned is that perceived risk of detection must be considered an important variable together with social norms with regard to the acceptance of undeclared work.

If these findings hold, a pure policy of deterrence may be considered problematic as social norms have an impact on undeclared work, too, but can be influenced less easily and less directly by short-term policy measures (Feld and Frey 2007). Long-term strategies that establish a social exchange relationship between the state and its citizens are much more difficult to find and to follow. The way in which the relationship between the state and its citizens shapes tax compliance and undeclared work is much more complex than it might appear at first sight, but, so far, the evidence does not point to increased deterrence as the *only* policy instrument to reduce undeclared work in addition to tax policy. Furthermore, as just mentioned, the implications for tax policy of the multivariate analyses in this study—represented by the effect of respondents' individually perceived marginal tax rates—are not clear-cut. Before any profound policy recommendation can be made, it is necessary to understand the complex interrelationship between deterrence and responsive regulation and how both lead to the establishment of a psychological tax contract as a social exchange relationship shaping tax morale. Much more depends on this than on mere short-term fiscal interests. It is a matter of civic culture, and thus it affects the foundation of the state in Germany.

Appendix

As the sample unit is the household, the probability of selection is not the same for any given individual. TNS Infratest Sozialforschung adjusts for this in a standard weighting procedure, which is also adjusted for non-response with regard to gender, age and region.

Appendix Tables 1 and 2 show the distributions of the respondents from each of the five surveys in 2001 and 2004–2007 compared to the population as a whole by gender and age. The figures in Appendix Table 2 are weighted, while the figures in Appendix Table 1 are not.

Before weights are applied to adjust the figures, the distribution by gender differs by up to about 3.5 percentage points, while weighting reduces the difference to about 0.5 percentage points. Weighting also adjusts for a considerable under-representation of men in the age group 25–44 years and an over-representation of the oldest age group, although, in 2007, weighting appears to have over-compensated to some extent as far as the age group 25–44 years is concerned.

Similarly, Appendix Tables 3 and 4 show the distribution by age and the two geographical regions, East and West Germany, before and after weighting. In Appendix Table 3 there are examples of significant differences between the unweighted sample distributions and the actual distributions of the German population, but these differences do not appear to be systematic, and as can be seen from Appendix Table 4, weighting reduces them except in the case of young women in East Germany in 2006 and 2007.

L.P. Feld and C. Larsen, *Undeclared Work, Deterrence and Social Norms*,
DOI 10.1007/978-3-540-87401-0,

Appendix Table 1 Respondents in the omnibus surveys compared with the whole population, by age and gender, 18 years and older, Germany, 2001 and 2004–2007, in percent, *unweighted*

Age	Respondents in the omnibus surveys			Whole population (1,000)		
	Men	Women %	Total	Men	Women %	Total
2001				31.12.2000		
18–24	9.7	9.0	9.3	10.3	9.3	9.8
25–44	34.6	38.9	37.0	40.3	35.6	37.8
45–59	24.3	22.0	23.0	24.3	22.4	23.3
60–64	10.9	7.6	9.1	8.7	8.4	8.6
65+	20.6	22.5	21.7	16.4	24.3	20.5
Total	100	100	100	100	100	100
%	44.8	55.2	100	48.2	51.8	100
No. of persons	2,756	3,398	6,154	32,201.4	34,558.0	66,759.4
2004				31.12.2004[a]		
18–24	8.7	7.7	8.2	10.5	9.5	10.0
25–44	29.6	32.6	31.3	37.6	33.7	35.6
45–59	21.8	21.5	21.6	24.9	23.1	24.0
60–64	9.8	9.2	9.4	7.8	7.6	7.7
65+	30.1	29.1	29.5	19.2	26.0	22.7
Total	100	100	100	100	100	100
%	44.8	55.2	100	48.4	51.6	100
No. of persons	1,083	1,332	2,415	32,745.0	34,927.1	67,672.1
2005				31.12.2004[a]		
18–24	9.2	8.7	8.9	10.5	9.5	10.0
25–44	28.4	32.4	30.6	37.6	33.7	35.6
45–59	26.4	25.5	25.9	24.9	23.1	24.0
60–64	9.6	8.4	8.9	7.8	7.6	7.7
65+	26.5	25.0	25.7	19.2	26.0	22.7
Total	100	100	100	100	100	100
%	46.2	53.8	100	48.4	51.6	100
No. of persons	1,092	1,270	2,362	32,745.0	34,927.1	67,672.1
2006				31.12.2006[b]		
18–24	10.0	7.3	8.5	10.5	9.5	10.0
25–44	26.9	31.3	29.3	36.0	32.6	34.3
45–59	21.2	26.1	23.9	26.4	24.6	25.5
60–64	10.2	8.0	9.0	6.4	6.2	6.3
65+	31.7	27.3	29.3	20.6	27.1	23.9
Total	100	100	100	100	100	100
%	45.9	54.1	100	48.5	51.5	100
No. of persons	1,122	1,324	2,446	32,995.8	35,077.1	68,072.9
2007				31.12.2006[b]		
18–24	12.1	11.0	11.5	10.5	9.5	10.0
25–44	26.4	32.2	29.6	36.0	32.6	34.3
45–59	22.8	23.6	23.3	26.4	24.6	25.5
60–64	8.1	6.2	7.1	6.4	6.2	6.3
65+	30.6	26.9	28.6	20.6	27.1	23.9

(continued)

Appendix Table 1 (continued)

Age	Respondents in the omnibus surveys			Whole population (1,000)		
	Men	Women %	Total	Men	Women %	Total
Total	100	100	100	100	100	100
%	45.1	54.9	100	48.5	51.5	100
No. of persons	553	673	1,226	32,995.8	35,077.1	68,072.9

Sources:
Surveys: The Rockwool Foundation Research Unit's Shadow Economy Surveys
Data for the whole population: Statistisches Bundesamt (Statistics Germany) (2002, 2006, 2008)
Note:
Due to rounding, the number of persons in Appendix Tables 1 and 2 may differ slightly from the number of persons in Appendix Tables 3 and 4
Due to rounding, the sum of the percentages may not be exactly 100
[a]31.12.2004 as the interviews in 2004 were carried out in the second half of the year and the interviews in 2005 were carried out in the first half of the year (see Appendix Tables 5 and 6)
[b]31.12.2006 as the interviews in 2006 were carried out in the second half of the year and the interviews in 2007 were carried out in the first half of the year (see Appendix Tables 5 and 6)

Appendix Table 2 Respondents in the omnibus surveys compared with the whole population, by age and gender, 18 years and older, Germany, 2001 and 2004–2007, in percent, *weighted*

Age	Respondents in the omnibus surveys			Whole population		
	Men	Women %	Total	Men	Women %	Total
2001				31.12.2000		
18–24	10.8	10.2	10.5	10.3	9.3	9.8
25–44	37.9	34.8	36.3	40.3	35.6	37.8
45–59	25.7	21.1	23.3	24.3	22.4	23.3
60–64	8.8	8.4	8.6	8.7	8.4	8.6
65+	16.8	25.5	21.3	16.4	24.3	20.5
Total	100	100	100	100	100	100
%	47.8	52.2	100	48.2	51.8	100
No. of persons	2,554.61	3,122.72	5,977.33	32,201.4	34,558.0	66,759.4
2004				31.12.2004[a]		
18–24	9.6	8.5	9.0	10.5	9.5	10.0
25–44	36.9	33.8	35.3	37.6	33.7	35.6
45–59	25.7	22.6	24.1	24.9	23.1	24.0
60–64	7.5	8.3	7.9	7.8	7.6	7.7
65+	20.3	26.8	23.7	19.2	26.0	22.7
Total	100	100	100	100	100	100

(continued)

Appendix Table 2 (continued)

Age	Respondents in the omnibus surveys			Whole population		
	Men	Women %	Total	Men	Women %	Total
%	47.7	52.3	100	48.4	51.6	100
No. of persons	1,128.33	1,236.76	2,365.09	32,745.0	34,927.1	67,672.1
2005				31.12.2004[a]		
18–24	9.6	11.0	10.3	10.5	9.5	10.0
25–44	35.9	30.0	32.8	37.6	33.7	35.6
45–59	26.4	23.8	25.1	24.9	23.1	24.0
60–64	8.3	6.9	7.5	7.8	7.6	7.7
65+	19.8	28.4	24.3	19.2	26.0	22.7
Total	100	100	100	100	100	100
%	47.8	52.2	100	48.4	51.6	100
No. of persons	1,130.26	1,235.17	2,365.43	32,745.0	34,927.1	67,672.1
2006				31.12.2006[b]		
18–24	10.9	9.6	10.3	10.5	9.5	10.0
25–44	37.0	31.9	34.3	36.0	32.6	34.3
45–59	24.0	23.1	23.5	26.4	24.6	25.5
60–64	7.9	8.8	8.4	6.4	6.2	6.3
65+	20.2	26.7	23.6	20.6	27.1	23.9
Total	100	100	100	100	100	100
%	48.2	51.8	100	48.5	51.5	100
No. of persons	1,143.2	1,229.6	2,372.79	32,995.8	35,077.1	68,072.9
2007				31.12.2006[b]		
18–24	13.3	11.4	12.3	10.5	9.5	10.0
25–44	30.0	29.0	29.5	36.0	32.6	34.3
45–59	28.8	25.0	26.8	26.4	24.6	25.5
60–64	6.6	7.0	6.8	6.4	6.2	6.3
65+	21.3	27.6	24.6	20.6	27.1	23.9
Total	100	100	100	100	100.0	100
%	47.9	52.1	100	48.5	51.5	100
No. of persons	575.79	626.92	1,202.71	32,995.8	35,077.1	68,072.9

Sources:
Surveys: The Rockwool Foundation Research Unit's Shadow Economy Surveys
Data for the whole population: Statistisches Bundesamt (Statistics Germany) (2002, 2006, 2008)
Note:
Due to rounding, the number of persons in Appendix Tables 1 and 2 may differ slightly from the number of persons in Appendix Tables 3 and 4
Due to rounding, the sum of the percentages may not be exactly 100
[a]31.12.2004 as the interviews in 2004 were carried out in the second half of the year and the interviews in 2005 were carried out in the first half of the year (see Appendix Tables 5 and 6)
[b]31.12.2006 as the interviews in 2006 were carried out in the second half of the year and the interviews in 2007 were carried out in the first half of the year (see Appendix Tables 5 and 6)

Appendix Table 3 Respondents in the omnibus surveys compared with the whole population, by age and region[a], 18 years and older, Germany, 2001 and 2004–2007, in percent, *unweighted*

Age	Respondents in the omnibus surveys			Whole population		
	West	East %	Total	West	East %	Total
2001				31.12.2000		
18–24	8.8	11.4	9.3	9.5	11.1	9.8
25–44[b]	37.8	33.5	37.0	38.3	35.6	37.8
45–59[b]	23.0	23.2	23.0	23.2	24.0	23.3
60–64	8.7	10.6	9.1	8.5	9.1	8.6
65+	21.8	21.3	21.7	20.6	20.3	20.5
Total	100	100	100	100	100	100
%	80.4	19.6	100	81.2	18.8	100
No. of persons	4,947	1,207	6,154	54,230.5	12,528.8	66,759.3
2004				31.12.2004[c]		
18–24	8.0	9.1	8.2	9.8	11.0	10.0
25–39[b]	23.3	16.2	22.0	25.7	22.4	25.1
40–59[b]	30.5	32.6	30.1	34.4	34.9	34.5
60–64	9.6	8.6	9.4	7.5	8.4	7.7
65+	28.7	33.6	29.5	22.6	23.4	22.7
Total	100	100	100	100	100	100
%	82.6	17.4	100	81.7	18.3	100
No. of persons	1,995	420	2,415	55,287.1	12,385.0	67,672.1
2005				31.12.2004[c]		
18–24	9.0	8.9	8.9	9.8	11.0	10.0
25–39[b]	21.7	19.5	21.2	25.7	22.4	25.1
40–59[b]	35.6	34.2	35.3	34.4	34.9	34.5
60–64	8.3	11.2	8.9	7.5	8.4	7.7
65+	25.5	26.3	25.7	22.6	23.4	22.7
Total	100	100	100	100	100	100
%	78.1	21.9	100	81.7	18.3	100
No. of persons	1,844	518	2,362	55,287.1	12,385.0	67,672.1
2006				31.12.2006[d]		
18–24	8.5	8.9	8.5	9.8	10.7	10.0
25–39[b]	20.2	17.2	19.6	24.2	21.3	23.7
40–59[b]	32.6	37.3	33.6	36.0	36.4	36.1
60–64	9.1	8.7	9.0	6.3	6.5	6.3
65+	29.7	27.9	29.3	23.7	25.1	23.9
Total	100	100	100	100	100	100
%	79.8	20.2	100	81.8	18.2	100
No. of persons	1,952	494	2,446	55,681.6	12,391.1	68,072.7
2007				31.12.2006[d]		
18–24	11.2	12.5	11.5	9.8	10.7	10.0
25–39[b]	21.3	21.1	21.3	24.2	21.3	23.7
40–59[b]	31.4	32.1	31.6	36.0	36.4	36.1
60–64	7.4	6.0	7.1	6.3	6.5	6.3
65+	28.6	28.3	28.6	23.7	25.1	23.9

(continued)

Appendix Table 3 (continued)

Age	Respondents in the omnibus surveys			Whole population		
	West	East %	Total	West	East %	Total
Total	100	100	100	100	100	100
%	78.4	21.6	100	81.8	18.2	100
No. of persons	961	265	1,226	55,681.6	12,391.1	68,072.7

Sources:
Surveys: The Rockwool Foundation Research Unit's Shadow Economy Surveys
Data for the whole population: Statistisches Bundesamt (Statistics Germany) (2002, 2006, 2008)
Note:
Due to rounding, the number of persons in Appendix Tables 1 and 2 may differ slightly from the number of persons in Appendix Tables 3 and 4
Due to rounding, the sum of the percentages may not be exactly 100
[a]The 2006 and 2008 editions of the Statistical Yearbook from Statistics Germany (Statistisches Bundesamt 2006, 2008) do not report separate figures for East and West Berlin. The proportions in the Statistical Yearbook from 2002 (Statistisches Bundesamt 2002) are used instead
[b]Age groups are slightly different in the 2002 edition of the Statistical Yearbook from Statistics Germany (Statistisches Bundesamt 2002) than in the 2006 and 2008 editions (Statistisches Bundesamt 2006, 2008)
[c]31.12.2004 as the interviews in 2004 were carried out in the second half of the year and the interviews in 2005 were carried out in the first half of the year (see Appendix Tables 5 and 6)
[d]31.12.2006 as the interviews in 2006 were carried out in the second half of the year and the interviews in 2007 were carried out in the first half of the year (see Appendix Tables 5 and 6)

Appendix Table 4 Respondents in the omnibus surveys compared with the whole population, by age and region,[a] 18 years and older, Germany, 2001 and 2004–2007, in percent, *weighted*

Age	Respondents in the omnibus surveys			Whole population (1,000)		
	West	East %	Total	West	East %	Total
2001					31.12.2000	
18–24	10.4	10.9	10.5	9.5	11.1	9.8
25–44[b]	36.3	36.3	36.3	38.3	35.6	37.8
45–59[b]	23.3	23.2	23.3	23.2	24.0	23.3
60–64	8.4	9.4	8.6	8.5	9.1	8.6
65+	21.6	20.2	21.3	20.6	20.3	20.5
Total	100	100	100	100	100	100
%	79.8	20.3	100	81.2	18.8	100
No. of persons	4,766.83	1,210.5	5,977.33	54,230.5	12,528.8	66,759.3
2004					31.12.2004[c]	
18–24	8.7	10.4	9.0	9.8	11.0	10.0
25–39[b]	26.0	24.4	25.7	25.7	22.4	25.1
40–59[b]	33.6	34.1	33.7	34.4	34.9	34.5
60–64	8.1	7.3	7.9	7.5	8.4	7.7
65+	23.7	23.9	23.7	22.6	23.4	22.7
Total	100	100	100	100	100	100
%	79.6	20.4	100	81.7	18.3	100
No. of persons	1,882.6	482.49	2,365.10	55,287.1	12,385.0	67,672.1

(continued)

Appendix Table 4 (continued)

Age	Respondents in the omnibus surveys			Whole population (1,000)		
	West	East %	Total	West	East %	Total
2005					31.12.2004[c]	
18–24	10.1	11.3	10.3	9.8	11.0	10.0
25–39[b]	24.0	22.3	23.7	25.7	22.4	25.1
40–59[b]	34.1	34.6	34.2	34.4	34.9	34.5
60–64	7.3	8.5	7.5	7.5	8.4	7.7
65+	24.5	23.3	24.3	22.6	23.4	22.7
Total	100	100	100	100	100	100
%	79.9	20.1	100	81.7	18.3	100
No. of persons	1,889.02	476.41	2,365.43	55,287.1	12,385.	67,672.1
2006					31.12.2006[d]	
18–24	9.4	13.7	10.3	9.8	10.7	10.0
25–39[b]	24.0	20.1	23.2	24.2	21.3	23.7
40–59[b]	34.7	34.5	34.6	36.0	36.4	36.1
60–64	8.4	8.2	8.4	6.3	6.5	6.3
65+	23.6	23.7	23.6	23.7	25.1	23.9
Total	100	100	100	100	100	100
%	79.7	20.3	100	81.8	18.2	100
No. of persons	1,891.52	481.27	2,372.79	55,681.6	12,391.1	68,072.7
2007					31.12.2006[d]	
18–24	11.8	14.5	12.3	9.8	10.7	10.0
25–39[b]	21.8	19.2	21.3	24.2	21.3	23.7
40–59[b]	35.1	34.9	35.1	36.0	36.4	36.1
60–64	6.9	6.3	6.8	6.3	6.5	6.3
65+	24.4	25.2	24.6	23.7	25.1	23.9
Total	100	100	100	100	100	100
%	79.7	20.3	100	81.8	18.2	100
No. of persons	957.91	244.80	1,202.71	55,681.6	12,391.1	68,072.7

Sources:
Surveys: The Rockwool Foundation Research Unit's Shadow Economy Surveys
Data for the whole population: Statistisches Bundesamt (Statistics Germany) (2002, 2006, 2008)
Note:
Due to rounding, the number of persons in Appendix Tables 1 and 2 may differ slightly from the number of persons in Appendix Tables 3 and 4
Due to rounding, the sum of the percentages may not be exactly 100
[a]The 2006 and 2008 editions of the Statistical Yearbook from Statistics Germany (Statistisches Bundesamt 2006, 2008) do not report separate figures for East and West Berlin. The proportions in the Statistical Yearbook from 2002 (Statistisches Bundesamt 2002) are used instead
[b]Age groups are slightly different in the 2002 edition of the Statistical Yearbook from Statistics Germany (Statistisches Bundesamt 2002) than in the 2006 and 2008 editions (Statistisches Bundesamt 2006, 2008)
[c]31.12.2004 as the interviews in 2004 were carried out in the second half of the year and the interviews in 2005 were carried out in the first half of the year (see Appendix Tables 5 and 6)
[d]31.12.2006 as the interviews in 2006 were carried out in the second half of the year and the interviews in 2007 were carried out in the first half of the year (see Appendix Tables 5 and 6)

Appendix Table 5 Proportion of the population in the 18–74 age group who has carried out undeclared work within the last year, by field period and gender, Germany, 2001 and 2004–2007

Field period	Men	Women	Total	Number of persons
April 2001	16.1	6.7	11.4	1,176
June 2001[a]	14.5	5.6	10.0	1,126
August 2001[b]	10.3	6.7	8.4	1,120
August 2001	15.0	6.9	10.8	1,138
October 2001	16.7	6.6	11.5	1,126
August 2004	12.2	3.6	7.8	1,077
October 2004	14.5	5.4	9.8	1,066
April 2005	12.9	8.0	10.4	1,078
June 2005	14.9	9.0	11.9	1,066
September 2006	9.0	5.3	7.2	1,083
October 2006	6.6	2.4	4.5	1,093
March 2007	15.8	3.8	9.7	1,096

Source:
The Rockwool Foundation Research Unit's Shadow Economy Surveys
Note:
The samples have been drawn at the household level, and a weight has been applied to make the sample representative as to gender and age distribution and other characteristics of the total population. The number of persons shown in the table is the actual number before the weight was applied
[a]31 May–28 June
[b]30 July–16 August

Appendix Table 6 Average time per week spent on undeclared work, 18–74-year-olds who have carried out undeclared work within the last year, by field period, Germany, 2001 and 2004–2007

Field period	Average time per week spent on undeclared work	Proportion of those who have carried out undeclared work who specify time spent on undeclared work	Number of persons who specify time spent on undeclared work
	Hours:minutes	%	
April 2001	10:16	65.8	76
June 2001[a]	8:27	50.7	54
August 2001[b]	8:39	64.0	54
August 2001	6:52	59.3	66
October 2001	6:43	58.2	62
August 2004	7:20	58.6	47
October 2004	7:40	42.9	56
April 2005	5:36	53.2	68
June 2005	7:32	58.4	66
September 2006	7:16	60.1	46
October 2006	4:59	55.6	28
March 2007	6:16	60.0	69

Source:
The Rockwool Foundation Research Unit's Shadow Economy Surveys
Note:
The samples have been drawn at the household level, and a weight has been applied to make the sample representative as to gender and age distribution and other characteristics of the total population. The number of persons shown in the table is the actual number before the weight was applied
[a]31 May–28 June
[b]30 July–16 August

Appendix Table 7 Logistic regression of the probability of having carried out undeclared work within the last year, *only socio-economic explanatory variables,* by gender, Germany, 2001 and 2004–2007

	Men				Women			
	Coefficient		Standard error	Marginal effect	Coefficient		Standard error	Marginal effect
Constant	−2.171	***	0.287		−3.410	***	0.468	
18–29	0.585	***	0.194	0.068	−0.058		0.240	−0.002
30–39	0.258		0.164	0.027	0.267		0.203	0.012
50–59	−0.325		0.200	−0.030	−0.152		0.233	−0.006
60–74	−0.690	***	0.249	−0.060	−0.774	*	0.420	−0.028
40–49								
Married	−0.092		0.134	−0.009	−1.045	***	0.166	−0.050
Not married								
Children <6	0.161		0.182	0.017	0.236		0.196	0.011
No children <6								
Self-employed	0.216		0.237	0.023	0.413		0.375	0.021
Skilled	0.447	**	0.176	0.049	0.681	**	0.296	0.038
Unskilled	0.077		0.244	0.008	0.601	***	0.228	0.030
Unemployed	−0.096		0.353	−0.009	0.655		0.430	0.036
Pensioner	−0.003		0.247	0.000	0.177		0.430	0.008
Student	−0.224		0.334	−0.021	1.006	**	0.407	0.065
Other	−0.126		0.303	−0.012	0.402		0.251	0.019
Salaried worker								
No education	−0.364	*	0.216	−0.033	−0.056		0.213	−0.002
Fachschule	0.400	**	0.182	0.045	0.414		0.252	0.020
Fachhochschule	−0.181		0.283	−0.017	0.377		0.319	0.018
Hochschule	−0.227		0.245	−0.021	0.481	*	0.249	0.024
Other	0.352		0.331	0.040	0.804		0.526	0.048
Student	−0.135		0.308	−0.013	0.520		0.406	0.027
Beruflich-betrieb-liche Ausbildung[a]								
€0–499[b]	0.608	**	0.287	0.074	0.775	*	0.403	0.037
€500–999	0.627	***	0.222	0.074	0.779	**	0.397	0.037
€1,000–1,499	0.142		0.188	0.015	0.638		0.395	0.032
€1,500–1,999	0.161		0.192	0.017	0.473		0.468	0.024
€2,000+								
Unemployment[c]	0.042	**	0.018	0.004	0.011		0.022	0.000
Not unemployed								
West Germany	−0.122		0.130	−0.013	0.073		0.180	0.003
East Germany								
Owner-occupier	0.163		0.120	0.017	0.229		0.145	0.010
Not owner-occup.								
2004	−0.094		0.159	−0.009	−0.389	*	0.201	−0.014
2005	−0.066		0.151	−0.007	0.271		0.183	0.012
2006	−0.716	***	0.161	−0.060	−0.635	***	0.226	−0.022
2007	0.127		0.229	0.013	−0.646	***	0.231	−0.021
2001								
Observations			6,045				7,142	
Log pseudo likelihood			−2,344.84				−1,352.44	

This appendix tableis summarized in Table 6.3

Source:

The Rockwool Foundation Research Unit's Shadow Economy Surveys

Note:

(continued)

Appendix Table 7 (continued)

	Men			Women		
	Coefficient	Standard error	Marginal effect	Coefficient	Standard error	Marginal effect

The dependent variable has the value 1 if the respondent has carried out undeclared work within the last 12 months and 0 otherwise
Significance levels: * 10%, ** 5%, *** 1%
The sample has been drawn at the household level, and a weight has been applied to make the sample representative as to gender and age distribution and other characteristics of the total population
[a]Includes apprentices
[b]Respondent's own monthly net income
[c]In months

Appendix Table 8 Logistic regression of the probability of having carried out undeclared work within the last year, *risk of detection included*, by gender, Germany, 2001 and 2004–2007

	Men				Women			
	Coefficient		Standard error	Marginal effect	Coefficient		Standard error	Marginal effect
Constant	−2.050	***	0.285		−3.154	***	0.466	
18–29	0.584	***	0.193	0.067	−0.102		0.242	−0.004
30–39	0.234		0.164	0.024	0.268		0.207	0.012
50–59	−0.340	*	0.201	−0.031	−0.168		0.234	−0.006
60–74	−0.711	***	0.250	−0.061	−0.781	*	0.416	−0.027
40–49								
Married	−0.072		0.135	−0.007	−1.064	***	0.166	−0.049
Not married								
Children <6	0.150		0.181	0.016	0.257		0.198	0.011
No children <6								
Self-employed	0.221		0.237	0.024	0.380		0.378	0.018
Skilled	0.459	***	0.177	0.050	0.658	**	0.296	0.035
Unskilled	0.104		0.244	0.011	0.597	***	0.229	0.029
Unemployed	−0.106		0.355	−0.010	0.559		0.433	0.028
Pensioner	0.011		0.249	0.001	0.142		0.426	0.006
Student	−0.255		0.338	−0.023	0.949	**	0.404	0.057
Other	−0.154		0.306	−0.014	0.351		0.251	0.016
Salaried worker								
No education	−0.368	*	0.216	−0.032	−0.057		0.214	−0.002
Fachschule	0.406	**	0.182	0.045	0.397		0.252	0.019
Fachhochschule	−0.192		0.284	−0.018	0.340		0.323	0.016
Hochschule	−0.261		0.241	−0.024	0.410		0.254	0.019

(continued)

Appendix Table 8 (continued)

	Men					Women				
	Coefficient		Standard error	Marginal effect		Coefficient		Standard error	Marginal effect
Other	0.363		0.329	0.041		0.817		0.514	0.048
Student	−0.201		0.316	−0.018		0.468		0.408	0.023
Beruflich-betriebliche Ausbildung[a]									
€0–499[b]	0.657	**	0.288	0.080		0.826	**	0.414	0.038
€500–999	0.655	***	0.223	0.077		0.830	**	0.408	0.039
€1,000–1,499	0.159		0.189	0.016		0.656		0.404	0.032
€1,500–1,999	0.160		0.192	0.016		0.463		0.476	0.022
€2,000+									
Unemployment[c]	0.043	**	0.018	0.004		0.014		0.023	0.001
Not unemployed									
West Germany	−0.119		0.130	−0.012		0.038		0.181	0.002
East Germany									
Owner-occupier	0.159		0.120	0.016		0.238		0.146	0.010
Not owner-occup.									
2004	−0.085		0.160	−0.008		−0.366	*	0.202	−0.013
2005	−0.027		0.151	−0.003		0.311	*	0.186	0.014
2006	−0.694	***	0.162	−0.058		−0.578	**	0.226	−0.020
2007	0.137		0.229	0.014		−0.591	**	0.232	−0.019
2001									
High risk[d]	−0.476	***	0.122	−0.045		−0.648	***	0.145	−0.025
Low risk									
Observations			6.045					7.142	
Log pseudo likelihood			−2328.641					−1,336.578	

This appendix table is summarized in Table 8.5

Source:

The Rockwool Foundation Research Unit's Shadow Economy Surveys

Note:

The dependent variable has the value 1 if the respondent has carried out undeclared work within the last 12 months and 0 otherwise

Significance levels: * 10%, ** 5%, *** 1%

The sample has been drawn at the household level, and a weight has been applied to make the sample representative as to gender and age distribution and other characteristics of the total population

[a]Includes apprentices

[b]Respondent's own monthly net income

[c]In months

[d]"High risk": The respondent perceives the risk of being detected and punished for carrying out undeclared work as very high or fairly high as opposed to the reference category "Low risk". The distribution of answers to this question is shown in Table 8.1. Missing values are set to the median value

Appendix Table 9 Logistic regression of the probability of having carried out undeclared work within the last year, *full deterrence included*, by gender, Germany, 2004–2007

	Men			Women		
	Coefficient	Standard error	Marginal effect	Coefficient	Standard error	Marginal effect
Constant	−1.688 ***	(0.414)		−2.892 ***	(0.619)	
18–29	0.696 ***	(0.264)	0.076	0.106	(0.351)	0.004
30–39	0.159	(0.232)	0.015	0.491 *	(0.298)	0.021
50–59	−0.318	(0.267)	−0.027	−0.063	(0.322)	−0.002
60–74	−0.725 *	(0.373)	−0.057	−0.800 *	(0.441)	−0.026
40–49						
Married	−0.048	(0.191)	−0.004	−1.030 ***	(0.219)	−0.044
Not married						
Children <6	0.135	(0.264)	0.013	0.415	(0.269)	0.018
No children <6						
Self-employed	0.092	(0.331)	0.009	0.256	(0.511)	0.011
Skilled	0.264	(0.246)	0.026	0.165	(0.458)	0.007
Unskilled	0.159	(0.330)	0.015	0.586 *	(0.315)	0.026
Unemployed	−0.297	(0.487)	−0.025	0.730	(0.565)	0.037
Pensioner	−0.099	(0.361)	−0.009	0.363	(0.434)	0.015
Student	−0.456	(0.460)	−0.036	0.606	(0.659)	0.029
Other	−0.393	(0.442)	−0.031	0.205	(0.339)	0.008
Salaried worker						
No education	−0.429	(0.315)	−0.034	−0.178	(0.317)	−0.006
Fachschule	0.450 *	(0.249)	0.047	0.428	(0.330)	0.019
Fachhochschule	−0.242	(0.392)	−0.020	−0.058	(0.473)	−0.002
Hochschule	−0.424	(0.346)	−0.034	0.392	(0.310)	0.017
Other	0.188	(0.433)	0.019	0.924	(0.645)	0.053
Student	−0.576	(0.403)	−0.043	−0.373	(0.684)	−0.012
Beruflich-betriebliche Ausbild[a]						
€0–499[b]	0.538	(0.388)	0.059	0.394	(0.496)	0.016
€500–999	0.486	(0.317)	0.051	0.565	(0.475)	0.023
€1,000–1,499	0.038	(0.260)	0.004	0.413	(0.462)	0.017
€1,500–1,999	0.085	(0.269)	0.008	0.214	(0.552)	0.009
€2,000+						
Unemployment[c]	0.042 *	(0.024)	0.004	−0.025	(0.030)	−0.001
Not unemployed						
West Germany	−0.313 *	(0.177)	−0.031	−0.170	(0.251)	−0.007
East Germany						
Owner-occupier	0.248	(0.174)	0.023	0.210	(0.197)	0.008
Not owner-occup.						
2005	0.024	(0.190)	0.002	0.673 ***	(0.232)	0.029
2006	−0.593 ***	(0.200)	−0.050	−0.152	(0.265)	−0.005
2007	0.220	(0.258)	0.021	−0.165	(0.276)	−0.006
2004						
High risk[d]	−0.346 **	(0.162)	−0.031	−0.682 ***	(0.191)	−0.025
Low risk						

(continued)

Appendix Table 9 (continued)

	Men			Women		
	Coefficient	Standard error	Marginal effect	Coefficient	Standard error	Marginal effect
Sanction prison[e]	−0.190	(0.308)	−0.016	−0.171	(0.394)	−0.006
Sanction fine	−0.181	(0.207)	−0.017	−0.182	(0.228)	−0.007
Sanction tax due						
Observations		3.460			4.078	
Log pseudo likelihood		−1,277.446			−729.634	

This appendix table is summarized in Table 8.6
Source:
The Rockwool Foundation Research Unit's Shadow Economy Surveys
Note:
The dependent variable has the value 1 if the respondent has carried out undeclared work within the last 12 months and 0 otherwise
Significance levels: * 10%, ** 5%, *** 1%
The sample has been drawn at the household level, and a weight has been applied to make the sample representative as to gender and age distribution and other characteristics of the total population
[a]Includes apprentices
[b]Respondent's own monthly net income
[c]In months
[d]"High risk": The respondent perceives the risk of being detected and punished for carrying out undeclared work as very high or fairly high as opposed to the reference category "Low risk". The distribution of answers to this question is shown in Table 8.1. Missing values are set to the median value
[e]The distribution of answers to this question is shown in Table 8.2. Missing values are set to the median value. Because questions about the perceived sanction for having carried out undeclared work were not asked until 2004, this and the rest of the regressions are without the data collected in 2001. The way of asking the questions about sanctions was adjusted several times from 2004 to 2006. See the notes to Table 8.2 or Table 8.4 for a detailed explanation. The latest version of the question is always used in the regressions. Therefore, in 2004 and 2005, the amount of evasion involved is 2,500 Euros while it is 10,000 Euros in 2006 and 2007

Appendix Table 10 Logistic regression of the probability of having carried out undeclared work within the last year, *full deterrence and marginal tax included*, by gender, Germany, 2004–2007

	Men				Women			
	Coefficient		Standard error	Marginal effect	Coefficient		Standard error	Marginal effect
Constant	−1.548	***	(0.443)		−3.094	***	(0.644)	
18–29	0.697	***	(0.263)	0.076	0.115		(0.353)	0.004
30–39	0.161		(0.232)	0.015	0.515	*	(0.296)	0.022
50–59	−0.321		(0.271)	−0.027	−0.047		(0.320)	−0.002
60–74	−0.718	*	(0.373)	−0.057	−0.803	*	(0.438)	−0.025
40–49								
Married	−0.049		(0.194)	−0.005	−1.029	***	(0.218)	−0.043
Not married								
Children <6	0.114		(0.262)	0.011	0.410		(0.270)	0.017
No children <6								
Self-employed	0.096		(0.331)	0.009	0.230		(0.508)	0.009

(continued)

Appendix Table 10 (continued)

	Men				Women			
	Coefficient		Standard error	Marginal effect	Coefficient		Standard error	Marginal effect
Skilled	0.276		(0.245)	0.027	0.165		(0.454)	0.006
Unskilled	0.166		(0.329)	0.016	0.597	*	(0.315)	0.026
Unemployed	−0.273		(0.487)	−0.023	0.636		(0.580)	0.030
Pensioner	−0.092		(0.366)	−0.008	0.287		(0.435)	0.011
Student	−0.462		(0.461)	−0.036	0.523		(0.661)	0.024
Other	−0.371		(0.450)	−0.030	0.096		(0.333)	0.004
Salaried worker								
No education	−0.427		(0.314)	−0.034	−0.183		(0.318)	−0.006
Fachschule	0.468	*	(0.250)	0.049	0.429		(0.329)	0.019
Fachhochschule	−0.239		(0.388)	−0.020	−0.085		(0.486)	−0.003
Hochschule	−0.407		(0.346)	−0.033	0.373		(0.306)	0.016
Other	0.208		(0.434)	0.021	0.840		(0.625)	0.045
Student	−0.525		(0.413)	−0.040	−0.410		(0.678)	−0.013
Beruflich-betriebliche Ausbild[a]								
€0–499[b]	0.532		(0.386)	0.058	0.362		(0.493)	0.014
€500–999	0.483		(0.314)	0.051	0.551		(0.472)	0.022
€1,000–1,499	0.034		(0.259)	0.003	0.394		(0.457)	0.016
€1,500–1,999	0.083		(0.266)	0.008	0.231		(0.550)	0.009
€2,000+								
Unemployment[c]	0.041	*	(0.024)	0.004	−0.024		(0.030)	−0.001
Not unemployed								
West Germany	−0.296	*	(0.178)	−0.029	−0.168		(0.251)	−0.006
East Germany								
Owner-occupier	0.241		(0.173)	0.022	0.215		(0.196)	0.008
Not owner-occupier								
2005	0.028		(0.191)	0.003	0.694	***	(0.229)	0.029
2006	−0.594	***	(0.201)	−0.050	−0.136		(0.263)	−0.005
2007	0.222		(0.263)	0.022	−0.123		(0.280)	−0.004
2004								
High risk[d]	−0.340	**	(0.161)	−0.030	−0.674	***	(0.190)	−0.024
Low risk								
Sanction prison[e]	−0.191		(0.310)	−0.016	−0.193		(0.399)	−0.007
Sanction fine	−0.183		(0.205)	−0.017	−0.186		(0.228)	−0.007
Sanction tax due								
Tax 0–19%[f]	−0.263		(0.271)	−0.022	0.625	*	(0.343)	0.028
Tax 40–49%	−0.252		(0.243)	−0.022	0.004		(0.365)	0.000

(continued)

Appendix Table 10 (continued)

	Men			Women		
	Coefficient	Standard error	Marginal effect	Coefficient	Standard error	Marginal effect
Tax 50–100%	−0.159	(0.204)	−0.015	0.248	(0.281)	0.009
Tax 20–39%						
Observations		3.460			4.078	
Log pseudo likelihood		−1,276.065			−725.914	

This appendix table is summarized in Table 9.3

Source:

The Rockwool Foundation Research Unit's Shadow Economy Surveys

Note:

The dependent variable has the value 1 if the respondent has carried out undeclared work within the last 12 months and 0 otherwise

Significance levels: * 10%, ** 5%, *** 1%

The sample has been drawn at the household level, and a weight has been applied to make the sample representative as to gender and age distribution and other characteristics of the total population

[a]Includes apprentices

[b]Respondent's own monthly net income

[c]In months

[d]"High risk": The respondent perceives the risk of being detected and punished for carrying out undeclared work as very high or fairly high as opposed to the reference category "Low risk". The distribution of answers to this question is shown in Table 8.1. Missing values are set to the median value

[e]The distribution of answers to this question is shown in Table 8.2. Missing values are set to the median value. Because questions about the perceived sanction for having carried out undeclared work were not asked until 2004, this and the rest of the regressions are without the data collected in 2001. The way of asking the questions about sanctions was adjusted several times from 2004 to 2006. See the notes to Table 8.2 or Table 8.4 for a detailed explanation. The latest version of the question is always used in the regressions. Therefore, in 2004 and 2005, the amount of evasion involved is 2,500 Euros while it is 10,000 Euros in 2006 and 2007

[f]The distribution of answers to this question is shown in Table 9.1. Missing values are set to the median value

Appendix Table 11 Logistic regression of the probability of having carried out undeclared work within the last year, *full deterrence, marginal tax and social norms included*, by gender, Germany, *missing set to median value*, 2004–2007

	Men				Women			
	Coefficient		Standard error	Marginal effect	Coefficient		Standard error	Marginal effect
Constant	−1.889	***	(0.481)		−3.668	***	(0.652)	
18–29	0.688	***	(0.264)	0.073	0.227		(0.344)	0.008
30–39	0.134		(0.238)	0.012	0.604	**	(0.291)	0.024
50–59	−0.322		(0.268)	−0.026	−0.054		(0.320)	−0.002
60–74	−0.747	**	(0.373)	−0.057	−0.831	*	(0.430)	−0.024
40–49								
Married	−0.060		(0.190)	−0.005	−1.080	***	(0.218)	−0.042
Not married								
Children <6	0.043		(0.265)	0.004	0.341		(0.275)	0.013
No children <6								
Self-employed	0.067		(0.335)	0.006	0.237		(0.516)	0.009
Skilled	0.265		(0.254)	0.025	0.293		(0.463)	0.011
Unskilled	0.122		(0.335)	0.011	0.595	*	(0.325)	0.024
Unemployed	−0.416		(0.482)	−0.032	0.766		(0.585)	0.036
Pensioner	−0.141		(0.367)	−0.012	0.354		(0.436)	0.013
Student	−0.404		(0.462)	−0.031	0.594		(0.665)	0.026
Other	−0.371		(0.458)	−0.029	0.158		(0.342)	0.006
Salaried worker								
No education	−0.338		(0.315)	−0.027	−0.110		(0.320)	−0.004
Fachschule	0.520	**	(0.253)	0.054	0.482		(0.329)	0.020
Fachhochschule	−0.178		(0.399)	−0.015	−0.027		(0.501)	−0.001
Hochschule	−0.327		(0.354)	−0.026	0.493		(0.308)	0.020
Other	0.195		(0.405)	0.019	0.871		(0.640)	0.044
Student	−0.410		(0.410)	−0.031	−0.420		(0.689)	−0.012
Beruflich-betriebliche Ausbild[a]								
€0–499[b]	0.572		(0.384)	0.061	0.463		(0.510)	0.017
€500–999	0.514		(0.317)	0.052	0.601		(0.484)	0.023
€1,000–1,499	0.063		(0.264)	0.006	0.474		(0.467)	0.018
€1,500–1,999	0.083		(0.273)	0.008	0.340		(0.563)	0.013
€2,000+								
Unemployment[c]	0.055	**	(0.023)	0.005	−0.024		(0.029)	−0.001
Not unemployed								
West Germany	−0.257		(0.178)	−0.024	−0.144		(0.244)	−0.005
East Germany								
Owner-occupier	0.242		(0.173)	0.021	0.263		(0.198)	0.009
Not owner-occup.								
2005	−0.027		(0.191)	−0.002	0.757	***	(0.219)	0.030
2006	−0.659	***	(0.207)	−0.052	−0.051		(0.258)	−0.002
2007	0.155		(0.262)	0.014	−0.035		(0.278)	−0.001
2004								
High risk[d]	−0.243		(0.164)	−0.021	−0.619	***	(0.190)	−0.021
Low risk								
Sanction prison[e]	−0.094		(0.316)	−0.008	−0.129		(0.401)	−0.004

(continued)

Appendix Table 11 (continued)

	Men				Women			
	Coefficient		Standard error	Marginal effect	Coefficient		Standard error	Marginal effect
Sanction fine	−0.157		(0.205)	−0.014	−0.179		(0.235)	−0.006
Sanction tax due								
Tax 0–19%[f]	−0.285		(0.265)	−0.023	0.562		(0.348)	0.023
Tax 40–49%	−0.189		(0.236)	−0.016	0.047		(0.372)	0.002
Tax 50–100%	−0.113		(0.200)	−0.010	0.280		(0.295)	0.009
Tax 20–39%								
Welfare without entitlement[g]	−0.234	**	(0.113)	−0.021	−0.266		(0.169)	−0.009
Carrying out udw	0.046		(0.048)	0.004	−0.094		(0.065)	−0.003
Private carries out udw for priv.	0.039		(0.044)	0.003	0.164	***	(0.053)	0.006
Firm carries out udw for private	0.100	**	(0.049)	0.009	0.072		(0.071)	0.002
Private carries out udw for firm	0.056		(0.075)	0.005	0.029		(0.087)	0.001
Firm carries out udw for firm	−0.094		(0.087)	−0.008	−0.033		(0.126)	−0.001
Tax evasion	0.049		(0.047)	0.004	0.049		(0.067)	0.002
Free riding on bus/ train								
Observations			3.460				4.078	
Log pseudo likelihood			−1,247.012				−708.919	

This appendix table is summarized in Table 10.3

Source:

The Rockwool Foundation Research Unit's Shadow Economy Surveys

Note:

The dependent variable has the value 1 if the respondent has carried out undeclared work within the last 12 months and 0 otherwise

Significance levels: * 10%, ** 5%, *** 1%

The sample has been drawn at the household level, and a weight has been applied to make the sample representative as to gender and age distribution and other characteristics of the total population

[a]Includes apprentices

[b]Respondent's own monthly net income

[c]In months

[d]"High risk": The respondent perceives the risk of being detected and punished for carrying out undeclared work as very high or fairly high as opposed to the reference category "Low risk". The distribution of answers to this question is shown in Table 8.1. Missing values are set to the median value

[e]The distribution of answers to this question is shown in Table 8.2. Missing values are set to the median value. Because questions about the perceived sanction for having carried out undeclared work were not asked until 2004, this and the rest of the regressions are without the data collected in 2001. The way of asking the questions about sanctions was adjusted several times from 2004 to 2006. See the notes to Table 8.2 or Table 8.4 for a detailed explanation. The latest version of the question is always used in the regressions. Therefore, in 2004 and 2005, the amount of evasion involved is 2,500 Euros while it is 10,000 Euros in 2006 and 2007

[f]The distribution of answers to this question is shown in Table 9.1. Missing values are set to the median value

[g]The distribution of answers to this question is shown in Table 10.1. Missing values are set to the median value

Appendix Table 12 Logistic regression of the probability of having carried out undeclared work within the last year, *full deterrence, marginal tax and social norms included*, by gender, Germany, *missing included as dummy*, 2004–2007

	Men				Women			
	Coefficient		Standard error	Marginal effect	Coefficient		Standard error	Marginal effect
Constant	−1.911	***	(0.505)		−3.404	***	(0.651)	
18–29	0.667	**	(0.275)	0.071	0.165		(0.372)	0.006
30–39	0.167		(0.247)	0.016	0.702	**	(0.302)	0.029
50–59	−0.427		(0.286)	−0.034	−0.106		(0.332)	−0.003
60–74	−0.831	**	(0.382)	−0.063	−0.627		(0.428)	−0.018
40–49								
Married	−0.024		(0.196)	−0.002	−1.035	***	(0.234)	−0.040
Not married								
Children <6	0.053		(0.271)	0.005	0.266		(0.300)	0.010
No children <6								
Self-employed	0.083		(0.349)	0.008	0.488		(0.522)	0.020
Skilled	0.315		(0.262)	0.030	0.429		(0.485)	0.017
Unskilled	0.194		(0.352)	0.019	0.684	**	(0.347)	0.028
Unemployed	−0.203		(0.507)	−0.017	1.010		(0.623)	0.052
Pensioner	−0.018		(0.372)	−0.002	0.371		(0.453)	0.013
Student	−0.271		(0.479)	−0.022	0.563		(0.758)	0.024
Other	−0.614		(0.521)	−0.044	0.177		(0.368)	0.006
Salaried worker								
No education	−0.344		(0.353)	−0.027	0.010		(0.349)	0.000
Fachschule	0.580	**	(0.263)	0.062	0.585	*	(0.343)	0.025
Fachhochschule	−0.068		(0.407)	−0.006	0.042		(0.527)	0.001
Hochschule	−0.270		(0.362)	−0.022	0.550	*	(0.327)	0.023
Other	0.069		(0.436)	0.006	0.969		(0.616)	0.050
Student	−0.336		(0.429)	−0.027	−0.086		(0.746)	−0.003
Beruflich-betriebliche Ausbild[a]								
€0–499[b]	0.654		(0.400)	0.072	0.335		(0.537)	0.012
€500–999	0.562	*	(0.331)	0.059	0.405		(0.501)	0.014
€1,000–1,499	0.102		(0.278)	0.009	0.343		(0.478)	0.012
€1,500–1,999	0.146		(0.282)	0.014	0.278		(0.570)	0.010
€2,000+								
Unemployment[c]	0.049	**	(0.024)	0.004	−0.035		(0.031)	−0.001
Not unemployed								
West Germany	−0.283		(0.183)	−0.027	−0.210		(0.249)	−0.007
East Germany								
Owner-occupier	0.312	*	(0.182)	0.028	0.204		(0.212)	0.007
Not owner-occup.								
2005	−0.036		(0.205)	−0.003	0.732	***	(0.244)	0.028
2006	−0.618	***	(0.216)	−0.050	−0.005		(0.281)	0.000
2007	0.254		(0.266)	0.025	−0.122		(0.306)	−0.004
2004								
High risk[d]	−0.263		(0.174)	−0.023	−0.769	***	(0.202)	−0.025
Missing risk	−0.182		(0.387)	−0.015	−0.873	**	(0.355)	−0.021
Low risk								
Sanction prison[e]	−0.197		(0.327)	−0.017	−0.143		(0.418)	−0.004
Sanction fine	−0.152		(0.219)	−0.014	−0.152		(0.248)	−0.005

(continued)

Appendix Table 12 (continued)

	Men				Women			
	Coefficient		Standard error	Marginal effect	Coefficient		Standard error	Marginal effect
Missing sanction	−0.140		(0.298)	−0.012	−0.526		(0.342)	−0.015
Sanction tax due								
Tax 0–19%[f]	−0.393		(0.275)	−0.031	0.584		(0.377)	0.023
Tax 40–49%	−0.091		(0.264)	−0.008	0.059		(0.452)	0.002
Tax 50–100%	−0.097		(0.210)	−0.009	0.337		(0.322)	0.011
Missing tax	−0.654	**	(0.307)	−0.048	0.052		(0.433)	0.002
Tax 20–39%								
Welfare without entitlement[g]	−0.208	*	(0.110)	−0.019	−0.182		(0.159)	−0.006
Carrying out udw	0.057		(0.051)	0.005	−0.069		(0.070)	−0.002
Private carries out udw for priv.	0.020		(0.045)	0.002	0.158	***	(0.057)	0.005
Firm carries out udw for private	0.111	**	(0.050)	0.010	0.058		(0.081)	0.002
Private carries out udw for firm	0.020		(0.072)	0.002	0.020		(0.104)	0.001
Firm carries out udw for firm	−0.093		(0.087)	−0.008	−0.061		(0.157)	−0.002
Tax evasion	0.051		(0.049)	0.005	0.008		(0.081)	0.000
Free riding on bus/ train								
Observations			3.124				3.659	
Log pseudo likelihood			−1.142.167				−630.094	

This appendix table is summarized in Table 10.3

Source:

The Rockwool Foundation Research Unit's Shadow Economy Surveys

Note:

The dependent variable has the value 1 if the respondent has carried out undeclared work within the last 12 months and 0 otherwise

Significance levels: * 10%, ** 5%, *** 1%

The sample has been drawn at the household level, and a weight has been applied to make the sample representative as to gender and age distribution and other characteristics of the total population

[a]Includes apprentices

[b]Respondent's own monthly net income

[c]In months

[d]"High risk": The respondent perceives the risk of being detected and punished for carrying out undeclared work as very high or fairly high as opposed to the reference category "Low risk". The distribution of answers to this question is shown in Table 8.1.

[e]The distribution of answers to this question is shown in Table 8.2. Because questions about the perceived sanction for having carried out undeclared work were not asked until 2004, this and the rest of the regressions are without the data collected in 2001. The way of asking the questions about sanctions was adjusted several times from 2004 to 2006. See the notes to Table 8.2 or Table 8.4 for a detailed explanation. The latest version of the question is always used in the regressions. Therefore, in 2004 and 2005, the amount of evasion involved is 2,500 Euros while it is 10,000 Euros in 2006 and 2007

[f]The distribution of answers to this question is shown in Table 9.1.

[g]The distribution of answers to this question is shown in Table 10.1. Due to the way these variables are constructed by division by the answer to the question about free ride on public transportation, it has not been possible to include missing values as dummy variables. Observations with missing values in questions about norms are therefore not included in the regressions in this table and the number of persons is smaller than in regressions where missing values are set to the median value of the answers from other respondents

Appendix Table 13 Logistic regression of the probability of having carried out undeclared work within the last year, *full deterrence, marginal tax and social norms included*, joint regressions for men and women, Germany, 2004–2007

	Missing set to the median value				Missing included as dummy variable			
	Coefficient		Standard error	Marginal effect	Coefficient		Standard error	Marginal effect
Constant	−2.815	***	(0.408)		−2.741	***	(0.429)	
Man	0.872	***	(0.134)	0.054	0.853	***	(0.144)	0.053
Woman								
18–29	0.453	**	(0.204)	0.031	0.421	*	(0.217)	0.029
30–39	0.175		(0.186)	0.011	0.223		(0.194)	0.014
50–59	−0.256		(0.210)	−0.014	−0.321		(0.227)	−0.018
60–74	−0.799	***	(0.283)	−0.041	−0.767	***	(0.289)	−0.040
40–49								
Married	−0.465	***	(0.139)	−0.029	−0.442	***	(0.146)	−0.028
Not married								
Children <6	0.210		(0.186)	0.014	0.207		(0.193)	0.014
No children <6								
Self-employed	0.131		(0.286)	0.008	0.181		(0.299)	0.012
Skilled	0.383	*	(0.213)	0.026	0.474	**	(0.223)	0.034
Unskilled	0.368		(0.229)	0.025	0.438	*	(0.237)	0.031
Unemployed	0.050		(0.383)	0.003	0.284		(0.400)	0.019
Pensioner	0.111		(0.281)	0.007	0.193		(0.284)	0.012
Student	0.141		(0.369)	0.009	0.187		(0.387)	0.012
Other	0.027		(0.264)	0.002	−0.055		(0.288)	−0.003
Salaried worker								
No education	−0.214		(0.217)	−0.012	−0.167		(0.243)	−0.010
Fachschule	0.537	***	(0.204)	0.039	0.608	***	(0.212)	0.046
Fachhochschule	−0.133		(0.314)	−0.008	−0.010		(0.319)	−0.001
Hochschule	0.012		(0.252)	0.001	0.075		(0.262)	0.005
Other	0.508		(0.372)	0.038	0.469		(0.397)	0.035
Student	−0.421		(0.359)	−0.021	−0.273		(0.370)	−0.015
Beruflich-betriebliche Ausbild[a]								
€0–499[b]	0.199		(0.274)	0.012	0.229		(0.288)	0.015
€500–999	0.315		(0.252)	0.020	0.302		(0.264)	0.020
€1,000–1,499	0.106		(0.223)	0.007	0.119		(0.234)	0.007
€1,500–1,999	0.123		(0.246)	0.008	0.162		(0.255)	0.010
€2,000+								

(continued)

Appendix Table 13 (continued)

	Missing set to the median value				Missing included as dummy variable			
	Coefficient		Standard error	Marginal effect	Coefficient		Standard error	Marginal effect
Unemployment[c]	0.033	*	(0.019)	0.002	0.026		(0.020)	0.002
Not unemployed								
West Germany	−0.243	*	(0.140)	−0.015	−0.282	*	(0.144)	−0.019
East Germany								
Owner-occupier	0.225	*	(0.130)	0.014	0.244	*	(0.137)	0.015
Not owner-occup.								
2005	0.226		(0.149)	0.014	0.216		(0.161)	0.014
2006	−0.467	***	(0.166)	−0.026	−0.418	**	(0.175)	−0.024
2007	0.090		(0.207)	0.006	0.152		(0.216)	0.010
2004								
High risk[d]	−0.386	***	(0.129)	−0.022	−0.425	***	(0.139)	−0.025
Missing risk					−0.348		(0.295)	−0.019
Low risk								
Sanction prison[e]	−0.115		(0.246)	−0.007	−0.211		(0.256)	−0.012
Sanction fine	−0.155		(0.158)	−0.010	−0.144		(0.169)	−0.009
Missing sanction					−0.284		(0.229)	−0.016
Sanction tax due								
Tax 0–19%[f]	0.043		(0.206)	0.003	−0.031		(0.214)	−0.002
Tax 40–49%	−0.134		(0.199)	−0.008	−0.078		(0.228)	−0.005
Tax 50–100%	−0.025		(0.160)	−0.001	−0.018		(0.168)	−0.001
Missing tax					−0.480	*	(0.246)	−0.025
Tax 20–39%								
Welfare without entitlement[g]	−0.226	**	(0.094)	−0.014	−0.183	**	(0.090)	−0.011
Carrying out udw	−0.018		(0.039)	−0.001	−0.000		(0.042)	0.000
Private carries out udw for priv.	0.090	***	(0.034)	0.005	0.074	**	(0.037)	0.005
Firm carries out udw for private	0.095	**	(0.038)	0.006	0.097	**	(0.041)	0.006
Private carries out udw for firm	0.046		(0.057)	0.003	0.024		(0.060)	0.001
Firm carries out udw for firm	−0.079		(0.072)	−0.005	−0.090		(0.076)	−0.005

(continued)

Appendix Table 13 (continued)

	Missing set to the median value			Missing included as dummy variable		
	Coefficient	Standard error	Marginal effect	Coefficient	Standard error	Marginal effect
Tax evasion	0.043	(0.038)	0.003	0.029	(0.040)	0.002
Free riding on bus/ train						
Observations		7.538			6.783	
Log pseudo likelihood		−1,999.242			−1,823.359	

This appendix table is summarized in Table 10.3
Source:
The Rockwool Foundation Research Unit's Shadow Economy Surveys
Note:
The dependent variable has the value 1 if the respondent has carried out undeclared work within the last 12 months and 0 otherwise
Significance levels: * 10%, ** 5%, *** 1%
The sample has been drawn at the household level, and a weight has been applied to make the sample representative as to gender and age distribution and other characteristics of the total population
[a]Includes apprentices
[b]Respondent's own monthly net income
[c]In months
[d]"High risk": The respondent perceives the risk of being detected and punished for carrying out undeclared work as very high or fairly high as opposed to the reference category "Low risk". The distribution of answers to this question is shown in Table 8.1.
[e]The distribution of answers to this question is shown in Table 8.2. Because questions about the perceived sanction for having carried out undeclared work were not asked until 2004, this and the rest of the regressions are without the data collected in 2001. The way of asking the questions about sanctions was adjusted several times from 2004 to 2006. See the notes to Table 8.2 or Table 8.4 for a detailed explanation. The latest version of the question is always used in the regressions. Therefore, in 2004 and 2005, the amount of evasion involved is 2,500 Euros while it is 10,000 Euros in 2006 and 2007
[f]The distribution of answers to this question is shown in Table 9.1.
[g]The distribution of answers to this question is shown in Table 10.1. Due to the way these variables are constructed by division by the answer to the question about free ride on public transportation, it has not been possible to include missing values as dummy variables. Observations with missing values in questions about norms are therefore not included in the regression in the right-hand side of this table and the number of persons is smaller than in the regressions where missing values are set to the median value of the answers from other respondents

References

Allingham, M. G., & Sandmo, A. (1972). Income tax evasion: A theoretical analysis. *Journal of Public Economics, 1*, 323–338.

Alm, J., Jackson, B. R., & McKee, M. (1992a). Estimating the determinants of taxpayer compliance with experimental data. *National Tax Journal, 45*, 107–114.

Alm, J., Jackson, B. R., & McKee, M. (1992b). Institutional uncertainty and taxpayer compliance. *The American Economic Review, 82*, 1018–1026.

Alm, J., Jackson, B. R., & McKee, M. (1993). Fiscal exchange, collective decision institutions and tax compliance. *Journal of Economic Behavior and Organization, 22*, 285–203.

Alm, J., McClelland, G. H., & Schulze, W. D. (1992c). Why do people pay taxes? *Journal of Public Economics, 48*, 21–38.

Alm, J., McClelland, G. H., & Schulze, W. D. (1999). Changing the social norm of tax compliance by voting. *Kyklos, 52*, 141–171.

Andreoni, J., Erard, B., & Feinstein, J. (1998). Tax compliance. *Journal of Economic Literature, 36*, 818–860.

Avenhaus, R., von Stengel, B., & Zamir, S. (1998). Inspection games. In R. J. Aumann & S. Hart (Eds.), *Handbook of game theory with economic applications* (Vol. 3, pp. 1947–1987). Amsterdam: Elsevier.

Becker, G. S. (1968). Crime and punishment: An economic approach. *Journal of Political Economy, 76*, 169–217.

Bilsdorfer, P. (2003). Die Entwicklung des Steuerstraf- und Steuerordnungswidrigkeitenrechts. *Neue Juristische Wochenschrift (NJW), 32*, 2281–2288.

Blackwell, C. (2010). A meta-analysis of incentive effects in tax compliance experiments. In J. Alm, J. Martinez-Vazquez, & B. Torgler (Eds.), *Developing alternative frameworks explaining tax compliance* (pp. 97–112). London: Routledge.

Boockmann, B., & Rincke, J. (2005). *Wirksamkeit der Bekämpfung der Schwarzarbeit durch die "Finanzkontrolle Schwarzarbeit": Empirische Untersuchung der Entwicklung der Schwarzarbeit und des hierauf bezogenen Bewusstseins- und Wertewandels – Machbarkeitsstudie –*. Mannheim: Abschlussbericht an das Bundesministerium der Finanzen, ZEW.

Engel, E., & Hines, J. R. (1999). Understanding tax evasion dynamics. NBER Working Paper No. 6903, NBER, Cambridge, MA.

Enste, D. H., Hülskamp, N., & Schäfer, H. (2009). *Familienunterstützende Dienstleistungen: Marktstrukturen Potenziale und Politikoptionen*. Köln: Deutscher Instituts-Verlag.

Eurobarometer (2007). *Undeclared work in the European Union*. Special Eurobarometer 284/ Wave 67.3. Requested by Directorate General Employment, Social Affairs and Equal Opportunities and coordinated by Directorate General Communication, Brussels.

Eurostat (2008). Databank at http://epp.eurostat.ec.europa.eu.

L.P. Feld and C. Larsen, *Undeclared Work, Deterrence and Social Norms*,
DOI 10.1007/978-3-540-87401-0,

Feige, E. L. (1989). *The underground economies: Tax evasion and information distortion.* Cambridge: Cambridge University Press.

Feld, L. P. & Frey, B. S. (2002a). The tax authority and the taxpayer: An exploratory analysis. Unpublished Manuscript, University of Zurich.

Feld, L. P., & Frey, B. S. (2002b). Trust breeds trust: How taxpayers are treated. *Economics of Governance, 3*, 87–99.

Feld, L. P., & Frey, B. S. (2005). Illegal, immoral, fattening or what?: How deterrence and responsive regulation shape tax morale. In F. Schneider & C. Bajada (Eds.), *Size, cause and consequences of the underground economy* (pp. 15–37). Aldershot: Ashgate.

Feld, L. P., & Frey, B. S. (2007). Tax compliance as the result of a psychological tax contract: The role of incentives and responsive regulation. *Law and Policy, 29*, 102–120.

Feld, L. P., & Larsen, C. (2005). *Black activities in Germany in 2001 and in 2004. A comparison based on survey data.* Study No. 12 from the Rockwool Foundation Research Unit, Copenhagen.

Feld, L. P., & Larsen, C. (2006). Strafen, Kontrollen und Schwarzarbeit: Einige Anmerkungen auf Basis von Befragungsdaten für Deutschland. *Jahrbuch Schattenwirtschaft, 1*, 81–107. and 211–213.

Feld, L. P., & Larsen, C. (2008). “Black” activities low in Germany in 2006. *News from the Rockwool Foundation Research Unit*, March 2008.

Feld, L. P., & Larsen, C. (2012). *Undeclared Work, Deterrence and Social Norms: The Case of Germany*. Berlin: Springer.

Feld, L. P., Schmidt, A. J., & Schneider, F. (2011). Deterrence policy and the size of the shadow economy in Germany: An institutional and empirical analysis. In: F. Schneider (Ed.), *Handbook on the shadow economy* (409–440). Cheltenham: Edward Elgar.

Feld, L. P., & Schneider, F. (2010). Survey on the shadow economy and undeclared earnings in OECD countries. *The German Economic Review, 11*, 109–149.

Feld, L. P., Torgler, B., & Dong, B. (2009). Coming closer? Tax morale, deterrence and social learning after German unification. Unpublished Manuscript, Ruprecht-Karls-University Heidelberg.

Feld, L. P., & Tyran, J.-R. (2002). Tax evasion and voting: An experimental analysis. *Kyklos, 55*, 197–222.

Fischer, C. M., Wartik, M., & Mark, M. M. (1992). Detection probability and taxpayer compliance: A review of the literature. *Journal of Accounting Literature, 11*, 1–46.

Frey, B. S. (1997a). *Not just for the money. An economic theory of personal motivation.* Cheltenham: Edward Elgar.

Frey, B. S. (1997b). A constitution for knaves crowds out civic virtues. *The Economic Journal, 107*, 1043–1053.

Frey, B. S., & Feld, L. P. (2002). Deterrence and morale in taxation: An empirical analysis. CESifo Working Paper No. 760, August 2002.

Frey, B. S., & Weck-Hannemann, H. (1984). The hidden economy as an ‘unobserved’ variable. *European Economic Review, 26*, 33–53.

Gneezy, U., & Rustichini, A. (2000). A fine is a price. *The Journal of Legal Studies, 29*, 1–17.

Goldstein, H. (1990). *Estimering af svart inntekt I Norge for 1988* (Estimation of Black Incomes in Norway for 1988). Arbejdsnotat no. 4/1990, Senter for anvendt forskning, Socialøkonomisk institute, Universitetet I Oslo, Oslo.

Güth, W., Levati, V., & Sausgruber, R. (2005). Tax morale and (de-) centralization: An experimental study. *Public Choice, 125*, 171–188.

Güth, W., & Mackscheidt, K. (1985). Die Erforschung der Steuermoral. Working Paper, University of Cologne.

Hvidtfeldt, C., Jensen, B., & Larsen, C. (2010). *Danskerne og det sorte arbejde.* Odense: University Press of Southern Denmark.

IAB (Institut für Arbeitsmarkt- und Berufsforschung). (2008). *IAB-Kurzbericht 13/2008.* Nürnberg: Bundesagentur für Arbeit.

Institut für Demoskopie (IfD) Allensbach (1975). Freizeitarbeit 1974. Studie im Auftrag der Kommission für wirtschaftlichen und sozialen Wandel, Allensbach.

Isachsen, A. J., & Strøm, S. (1985). The size and growth of the hidden economy in Norway. *The Review of Income and Wealth, 31*, 21–38.

Kanniainen, V., Pääkönen, J., & Schneider, F. (2004). *Fiscal and ethical determinants of shadow economy: Theory and evidence, mimeo*. Linz: Johannes-Kepler University.

Kirchgässner, G. (1983). Size and development of the West German shadow economy, 1955–1980. *Zeitschrift für die gesamte Staatswissenschaft (ZgS)/Journal of Institutional and Theoretical Economics (JITE), 139*, 197–214.

Kirchler, E. (2007). *The economic psychology of tax behaviour*. Cambridge: Cambridge University Press.

Kleven, H. J., Knudsen, M. B., Kreiner, C. T., Pedersen, S., & Saez, E. (2011). Unwilling or unable to cheat? Evidence from a tax audit experiment in Denmark. *Econometrica, 79*, 651–692.

Körner, M., & Strotmann, H. (2004) (in cooperation with Feld, L. P., & Schneider, F.). *Steuermoral – Das Spannungsfeld von Freiwilligkeit der Steuerzahlung und Regelverstoß durch Steuerhinterziehung*. Studie im Auftrag des Bundesministeriums der Finanzen, Institut für Angewandte Wirtschaftsforschung, Tübingen.

Lackó, M. (1998). The hidden economies of Visegrad countries in international comparison: A household electricity approach. In L. Halpern & C. Wyplosz (Eds.), *Hungary: Towards a market economy* (pp. 128–152). Cambridge: Cambridge University Press.

Lamnek, S., Olbrich, G., & Schäfer, W. J. (2000). *Tatort Sozialstaat: Schwarzarbeit. Leistungsmissbrauch, Steuerhinterziehung und ihre (Hinter)Gründe*. Opladen: Leske and Budrich.

Langfeldt, E. (1984a). The unobserved economy in the Federal Republic of Germany. In E. L. Feige (Ed.), *The unobserved economy* (pp. 236–260). Cambridge: Cambridge University Press.

Langfeldt, E. (1984b). *Die Schattenwirtschaft in der Bundesrepublik Deutschland* (Kieler Studien 191). Tübingen: Mohr Siebeck.

Larsen, C. (2002). Underdeklaration af personlig indkomst måt ved sammenligning af dansk skatte- og nationalregnskabsstatistik (Unreported Personal Income Estimated by Examining Discrepancies between Danish National Accounts and Tax Statistics). Mimeographed, Institute of Economics, University of Copenhagen, Copenhagen.

Licht, A. N. (2008). Social norms and the law: Why peoples obey the law. *Review of Law & Economics, 4*, 715–750.

Lippert, O., & Walker, M. (Eds.). (1997). *The underground economy: Global evidences of its size and impact*. Vancouver, BC: The Frazer Institute.

Lyssiotou, P., Pashardes, P., & Stengos, T. (2004). Estimates of the black economy based on consumer demand approaches. *The Economic Journal, 114*, 622–640.

Mummert, A., & Schneider, F. (2001). The German shadow economy: Parted in a United Germany? *Finanzarchiv, 58*, 286–316.

OECD. (2002). *Measuring the non-observed economy. A handbook*. Paris: OECD.

Ognedal, T., Goldstein, H., Hansen, W. G., & Strøm, S. (2002). Svart arbeid fra 1980 til 2001 (Black Activities in Norway from 1980 to 2001). Oslo: Ragnar Frisch Centre for Economic Research.

Pedersen, S. (2003). *The shadow economy in Germany, Great Britain and Scandinavia: a measurement based on questionnaire surveys*. Study No. 10. Copenhagen: The Rockwool Foundation Research Unit.

Pickhardt, M., & Sardà Pons, J. (2006). Size and scope of the underground economy in Germany. *Applied Economics, 38*, 1707–1713.

Pommerehne, W. W., & Frey, B. S. (1992). The effects of tax administration on tax morale. Unpublished Manuscript, University of Zurich.

Pommerehne, W. W., & Weck-Hannemann, H. (1996). Tax rates, tax administration and income tax evasion in Switzerland. *Public Choice, 88*, 161–170.

Reinganum, J. F., & Wilde, L. L. (1986). Equilibrium verification and reporting policies in a model of tax compliance. *International Economic Review, 27*, 739–760.

Schanze, E. (1995). Hare and hedgehog revisited: The regulation of markets that have escaped regulated markets. *Journal of Institutional and Theoretical Economics (JITE), 151*, 162–176.

Schneider, F. (2004a). Shadow economies around the world: What do we really know? Unpublished Manuscript, University of Linz.

Schneider, F. (2004b). *Arbeit im Schatten: Wo Deutschlands Wirtschaft wirklich wächst.* Wiesbaden: Gabler.

Schneider, H. (2004c). Steuerhinterziehung aus Perspektive der Marketingwissenschaft. Eine empirische Analyse zu den Ursachen der Steuerhinterziehung von Privatpersonen. In R. Robert & P. Kevenhörster (Eds.), *Kommunen in Not: Aufgaben- und Finanzverantwortung in Deutschland* (pp. 271–295). Münster: Waxmann Verlag.

Schneider, F. (2010). *The influence of the economic crisis on the underground economy in Germany and other OECD-countries in 2010: A (further) increase.* Johannes Kepler University of Linz. Revised version January 26, 2010, available at www.econ.jku.at/schneider/.

Schneider, F., & Enste, D. (2000). Shadow economies: Size, causes, consequences. *Journal of Economic Literature, 38*, 77–114.

Schneider, F., & Enste, D. (2002). *The shadow economy: An international study.* Cambridge: Cambridge University Press.

Scholz, J. T., & Lubell, M. (2001). Cooperation, reciprocity and the collective action heuristic. *American Journal of Political Science, 45*, 160–178.

Skatteministeriet, Told- og Skattestyrelsen (Ministry of Taxation) (2001). *Ligningsvejledning Erhvervsdrivende 2000* (Tax Assessment Manual Self-Employed 2000), Copenhagen.

Slemrod, J. (2007). Cheating ourselves: The economics of tax evasion. *Journal of Economic Perspectives, 21*(1), 25–48.

Slemrod, J., Blumenthal, M., & Christian, C. W. (2001). Taxpayer response to an increased probability of audit: Evidence from a controlled experiment in Minnesota. *Journal of Public Economics, 79*, 455–483.

Slemrod, J., & Yitzhaki, S. (2002). Tax avoidance, evasion and administration. In A. J. Auerbach & M. Feldstein (Eds.), *Handbook of public economics, Vol. 3* (pp. 1423–1470). Amsterdam: North-Holland.

Statistisches Bundesamt (Statistics Germany) (2002). *Statistisches Jahrbuch 2002 für die Bundesrepublik Deutschland* (Statistical Yearbook 2002), Wiesbaden.

Statistisches Bundesamt (Statistics Germany) (2006). *Statistisches Jahrbuch 2006 für die Bundesrepublik Deutschland* (Statistical Yearbook 2006), Wiesbaden.

Statistisches Bundesamt (Statistics Germany) (2007). *Statistisches Jahrbuch 2007* (Statistical Yearbook 2007), Wiesbaden.

Statistisches Bundesamt (Statistics Germany) (2008) *Statistisches Jahrbuch 2008* (Statistical Yearbook 2008), Wiesbaden.

Statistisches Bundesamt (Statistics Germany) (2009). *Statistisches Jahrbuch 2009* (Statistical Yearbook 2009), Wiesbaden.

Thomas, J. (1999). Quantifying the black economy: Measurement without theory yet again. *The Economic Journal, 109*, F381–F387.

Torgler, B. (2002). Speaking to theorists and searching for facts: Tax morale and tax compliance in experiments. *Journal of Economic Surveys, 16*, 657–683.

Torgler, B. (2003). *Tax morale: Theory and empirical analysis of tax compliance.* Ph.D. Thesis, University of Basel.

Torgler, B. (2007). *Tax compliance and tax morale: A theoretical and empirical analysis.* Cheltenham: Edward Elgar.

Tyran, J. R., & Feld, L. P. (2006). Achieving compliance when legal sanctions are non-deterrent. *The Scandinavian Journal of Economics, 108*, 135–156.

Viby Mogensen, G. (2003). *Skattesnyderiets historie. Udviklingen i underdeklarationen i Danmark i 1900-tallet* (The History of Tax Evasion. The Development of Tax Evasion i Denmark in the 20th Century). Odense: Syddansk Universitetsforlag.

Viby Mogensen, G., Kvist, H. K. Körmendi, E. & Pedersen, S. (1995). *The Shadow Economy in Denmark 1994: Measurement and Results*. Study No. 3. Copenhagen: The Rockwool Foundation Research Unit.

Weck, H. (1983). *Schattenwirtschaft: Eine Möglichkeit zur Einschränkung der öffentlichen Verwaltung? Eine ökonomische Analyse*. Frankfurt: Peter Lang.

Weck-Hannemann, H., & Pommerehne, W. W. (1989). Einkommensteuerhinterziehung in der Schweiz: Eine empirische Analyse. *Schweizerische Zeitschrift für Volkswirtschaft und Statistik, 125*, 515–556.

Weck-Hannemann, H., Pommerehne, W. W., & Frey, B. S. (1984). *Schattenwirtschaft*. München: Vahlen.

Williams, C. C., Horlings, E., & Renooy, P. (2008). Tackling undeclared work in the European Union. Research report, European Foundation for the Improvement of Living and Working Conditions, Dublin.

WVS/EVS (2009). World and European values surveys 1981–2008. World Values Survey Association and European Values Study Group (www.worldvaluessurvey.org).

Index

L.P. Feld and C. Larsen, *Undeclared Work, Deterrence and Social Norms*,
DOI 10.1007/978-3-540-87401-0, © Springer-Verlag Berlin Heidelberg 2012

R

S

T

U

V

W